UNPACKING ONE ITEM AT A TIME

WHAT'S IN YOUR BAG?

UNPACKING ONE ITEM AT A TIME

UNPACKING ONE ITEM AT A TIME

WHAT'S IN YOUR BAG?

UNPACKING ONE ITEM AT A TIME

WILLIAM MICHAEL BARBEE

Copyright © 2018

All rights reserved. Except as permitted under the U.S. Copyright Act of 1976, no part of this publication may be reproduced, distributed, or transmitted in any form or by any means, or stored in a database or retrieval system, without the prior written permission of the publisher.

www.williammichaelbarbee.com

Printed in the United States of America

First Edition: February 2018

Book cover photographer: LaDonna P. Young

www.ladonnaimages.com

The publisher is not responsible for websites or their content that are not owned by the publisher.

Library of Congress Cataloging-in-Publication Data

ISBN   9781548482244

Editor: Kimberly Shamberger

Proof Reader: Leslie D. Cleveland

THIS BOOK IS DEDICATED TO:

RODNEY MAURICE GILBERT
Artistic Innovator, Mentor and Friend who supported me through much of my personal and professional artistic development. He taught me to value each day as though it was my last. *Gone too soon...*

BISHOP EVELYN COLSON WILLIAMS-GORDON
Educator, Pastor, Visionary, Aunt and Godmother who seeded into my life from the very beginning. She was the most loving and giving spirit that I have ever known.
Unselfish with her giving, she is the personification of philanthropy. *My Angel...*

ELETA J. CALDWELL
Visual Artist, Educator, Godmother and Friend who protected me from myself before I understood the ramifications of my actions. She guided me through many of my life challenges. *My Love....*

DEITRA LONG-DAVIS
Businesswoman, Matriarch, and Loving Cousin who found time to often call, encourage, provide love, and pray for me. She was always sweet and kept me close in her heart. It's the positive energy that she emits from her spirit that encourages me to be my best. *My Friend...*

UNPACKING ONE ITEM AT A TIME

CONTENTS

FOREWORD		xi
INTRODUCTION		1
Chapter 1:	Love	5
Chapter 2:	A Letter To Him	49
Chapter 3:	Forgiveness	81
Chapter 4:	Fear	103
Chapter 5:	Inner Voice	123
Chapter 6:	Masking	149
Chapter 7:	Embracing Change	173
Chapter 8:	Acts of Service	197
ABOUT THE AUTHOR		219
ACKNOWLEDGEMENTS		221

x

UNPACKING ONE ITEM AT A TIME

FOREWORD

I have always strived to become the adult I needed when I was 8 years old; someone steady, loving and generous. I wanted someone to care for the awkward and insecure boy I was, and on occasion still am. It was 1969 and my little world and the world at large was at war, there were neighborhood riots, and assassinations seemed out of control. The antidote then and now is love and forgiveness. The 8-year-old needs love and forgiveness, and the adult needs to give it to himself and others.

While I have had varying degrees of success in this aspiration, it has always been a worthy journey and one that has left me better off. So, it is with William Michael Barbee and his enlightening exploration of his past, and his reconciliation with those who loved him and more importantly himself, that we like Mike will never complete our journey. However, it is one we all must take.

Knowing and understanding yourself, as well as your heritage is vital for living a full life. By knowing, I don't mean dwelling in it, I mean understanding it for what it is. This includes the love, the family, the community, the church, the human failings, the violence, and the fire. As Mike would say, *"it's all in your bag."* As children, we don't have many choices as to what gets put in our bag, but as adults we get to decide what stays, what goes, and what gets added.

What stays is the love of our family, as flawed as it may have been. What stays is the love of neighbors and mentors who supported us, because that is what adults do, and that's what their community has taught them.

What goes? The anger at those whose best fell short of the glory; the disillusionment with the church that claimed to be gospel, but was mostly pews emphasizing the sin rather than the joy of a relationship with God; the guilt towards our adolescent self, the young person who was awkward, self-absorbed and didn't have a clue. By goes I don't mean to deny it, I mean understand it for what it was; our past, not our today and certainly not our future.

What gets added? The spiritual sense that our world is guided by a higher power and we sure as hell are not it. That's what Mike's mom and the church ladies would call humility. The love of oneself, not a vain love, but an acceptance of one's self. The ability to love others and accept love in return. Understanding that leadership of self, others, and the greater community begins with service.

I have a better sense of these things after reading Mike's *"What's In Your Bag?"* The learning never ends. Mike and I grew up about 10 miles apart, but in completely different worlds. Our ancestors came over in very different boats. We never ventured into each other's neighborhoods. I am struck by how little that seems to matter. It doesn't matter because as humans and children of God, we have far more in common than the elements of our past that might distinguish us. We all have basically the same *"bag."* I think you will develop a better sense of *what's in your bag* when you read this worthy composition.

Robert N. Davison, MA, LPC
Chief Executive Officer
Mental Health Association of Essex and Morris, Inc.

WHAT'S IN YOUR BAG?
UNPACKING ONE ITEM AT A TIME

INTRODUCTION

WHAT'S IN YOUR BAG is a rhetorical question that I pose to everyone. Somewhere in my psyche, I'm forever wondering how to better the him in me. I have become preoccupied with trying to understand the pathology of the things that I do. As I study my pathology, I cannot separate the fact that my African lineage has been filled with love, trust, abuse, abandonment, compassion and every other emotion that one can imagine. Being a product of African descent, I've noticed that historically we have communal spirits. We have an innate need to be social with others. It matters not whether it's a stranger or a friend. We gravitate towards community.

How often have you heard the African Proverb, *"It takes a village to raise a child?"* That proverb has been the cornerstone of many cultures throughout the world. Within its fabric, there are many participants who have kept our villages together. Being a product of Africans who are generationally embedded in the United States, I've come to realize that our villages are falling apart at the seams. Historically, our very families have been the focus of governmental systematic attacks that have deteriorated the structural, emotional and spiritual seams that have kept us together. Until we have honest dialogue that addresses the issues; restore structure; identify our purpose, and reinstitute love as a foundation of our community, then will we begin to see positive change.

It was my dad who often gave me lessons on my history as an American who is of African descent. He wanted me to have a clear understanding of who I was in society. He always told me that the history books that we studied in our classrooms were filled with many misrepresentations, as well as having intentionally voided stories. He explained the historical beauty of who we were as Kings and Queens of the Nubian Kingdoms; and how we were burdened by atrocities at the hands of others. He would say, *"You can't possibly know where you're going if you don't know where you come from."* While my Dad gave me this rich history of who we are as a people, it would take professional psychological help for me to understand who I am as a man.

Often, I am reminded of Clinical Psychologist John Bradshaw's *Infancy Exercise* where he says, *"Writing a letter to the child that lives within you helps you to finish the unfinished, so that you can go on with your life."* We all have a child who lives within us that occupies our adult bodies. In many cases, those children have had to bare the burdens of our unresolved issues into adulthood. In one example, Dr. Bradshaw uses a 3 year old child who was sexually abused. He said that they will act *"age inappropriate or have knowledge that's inappropriate to their age, it's the only way that the child has to express themselves."* Through this example, he's showing us the pathology of our past while giving us an understanding of how we perform in our present. Through his many techniques of channeling the child within, and my personal sessions with forensic psychotherapist Shelly Neiderbach, who showed me my *Invisible Wounds*; I was able to trace my emotional scars and begin to heal.

While this may be the method that I used for healing and understanding my thought process, it is also my recommended process to all who seek to enrich their lives by growing mentally, emotionally, and spiritually. If you were to take my story, which is comprised of so many of your stories, you'll find that we all carry bags of DNA; with a lineage of good and bad items that range from love to atrocities. This book is not designed to be a feel good experience for you. It is intended for you to become inspired to live beyond your fears, and explore the possibilities of forgiveness and love so that you can stop functioning and begin living. It is my hope that once you read this book and study the methods that I used to heal my soul and spirit, you too will be free. Make sure that you pass it on to someone else so that they can begin their process of healing.

William Michael Barbee

CHAPTER 1

LOVE

UNPACKING ONE ITEM AT A TIME

Love's complexity is that it is so simple.

How do you define love? Is it merely an emotion that we attach positive values to? Or, is it an action that leads to positive results? The ancient Greeks have used 7 words to describe love, each having a different meaning. Eros is the God of fertility. Philia is based on friendships. Storge is based on the love of unity that binds the family together. Ludus describes a more playful love. Agape for Christians is the highest form of love. Pragma describes the mature love that's longstanding. Finally, Philautia focuses on the love of self. These Greek terms for love have been used for centuries as the centerpieces, foundations, and theories by many of our great philosophers. In this chapter I will attempt to share my personal views on how some of these forms of love have impacted my life.

The older I become, the more introspective I am on my understanding of love. I've heard the word love throughout my life's journey. Some have defined it as the ultimate pinnacle of righteousness. They say God is love. How often have you heard people say, *"I love you"* without having any emotional or spiritual connection to the person they're speaking to? It is because of that disconnect, along with others that has led me to believe that while it's a simple word, it has many facets. It is also why it's imperative that I seek a better understanding of what it means to me.

I've chosen to reexamine the love that I experienced within my past relationships. I needed to have a better understanding if my love experiences were based solely on my desires and perceptions of what I wanted, versus the other person's experiences of what they wanted to share with me. I've come to accept that somewhere in the middle lies the truth of both of our experiences. Some of my relationships needed to have expiration dates on them. The energy that I exerted to maintain them could have been placed in other more meaningful ones. Some of those relationships were built on genuine shared bonds that we both sought. They were either for comfort, similar interests, mutual affiliations, convenience; or how we both were going to benefit from the other. To my surprise, I realized that I had fewer relationships that were built on pure love.

Before I can break down the relational love that I believed I shared with others, I needed to first define what love means to me based on my understanding of the Greek philosophers' theories. I began to look at Pragma Love. By definition, it involves the idealism of love that I would desire with another. This form of love intrigued me because of its focus on the important traits that one would look for in a relationship. I can spend a lot of time just thinking about how my ideal mate should look, sound and even feel. However, not often enough can I honestly say that I used the same amount of time and energy to study the ideal traits that I would desire to possess within myself. If I truly believed that I was the most important person in the universe, then why was I not in relationship with myself? The fact that I spent a lifetime chasing external forces to satisfy my internal needs speaks to my lack of understanding of how to love myself. It would take me nearly a lifetime to fully appreciate the value and importance of self-love and why the Greek Philautia Love is so important to me.

Recently, I had to dig deep within my Philautia Love while making a major business decision. Philautia can be seen as an unhealthy or healthy expression of love. In its negative, unhealthy form, it is extreme self-love. It's the selfishness that wants pleasures, fame, and fortune beyond what one needs. Contrarily, its positive expression is a deep unconditional love that I have for myself while considering everything and everyone around me. Having healthy Philautia, one would have displayed forms of forgiveness, self-compassion and a balance of empathy. Within Philautia, I'm able to accept the positive growth that comes with my public degrees of transparency, while being content that my dark areas may be exposed. An example of this love can be seen in how I valued my integrity after choosing to walk away from something that I also valued; my high profile position within a newly formed corporation. At face value, the company had the potential of producing millions and millions of dollars. When I agreed to join, my decision wasn't influenced solely by the potential of making a lot of money for myself. My main goal in accepting the position was based on my belief in myself, and that I possessed the ability to build success upon another person's ideas and dreams. I was confident in my abilities. I knew that I possessed the wherewithal to bring structure to this organization.

Amongst my many duties and responsibilities, I worked diligently alongside the founder of the company. Despite my knowledge, expertise, and experience in business, I had to work closely with someone whose leadership skills were not on par with mine. What he possessed was an ability to get people to buy into an idea and work for free. While working closely with him, I noticed that he and I did not share common ethical, moral, or religious ideologies. Not that it was a deal breaker, because it wasn't. I would notice him having extreme mood swings when dealing with people who worked for him or disagreed with his position on an issue. Due to his rapidly changing mood swings, it brought more attention to his lack of morals and ethics. He made promises to random people without displaying the desire to honor any of the promises that he made. This, along with other bad traits became routine methods of all of his business dealings with everyone.

Needless to say, I found myself in a catch 22. If I were to keep quiet and go along with his program, I would likely make a few million dollars. If I spoke out against the way he did business and his lack of ethics, I would surely ruffle his feathers and lose the possibility of future earnings. What I chose to do was to throw caution to the wind and stand on my integrity. I began to ruffle his feathers and let him know that his techniques were not acceptable business practices. To my surprise, he began to listen to me. He even went further and told me about where he thought the origins of his bad behavior were rooted. Whenever he spoke about issues that bothered him, he'd run back to his childhood memories and make references to how badly he was treated by those whose responsibility was to love him. He practically told me how he had to raise himself while making good and bad choices that got him from point A to point B.

In spite of the challenges that he faced, he is one of the most generous and empathetic individuals that I have had the honor of knowing. He had a charm and protected vulnerable side that

I truly came to love. I've seen firsthand how he fed, clothed, bought vehicles, and paid for room and board for individuals that he cared about. It was nothing for him to fix and repair anything that you needed done. Even with all of these commendable traits, he still lacked the ability to feel content with allowing his vulnerabilities to show. He saw outward expressions of emotions as signs of weakness. Therefore, he masked his fears by expressing himself outwardly through bullying and abusive behaviors to those who he could control. The closer our relationship became, the more I began to question him about the dual personalities that he displayed. On one hand, he's this phenomenal guy who will give you the shirt off of his back. On the other hand, he's this rude, cocky, and overly insecure person.

He would often sit in my office and cry while asking me to read this chapter on *love* and the one on *forgiveness*. Jokingly, he called me his therapist. He reflected on his horrible childhood and how it negatively impacted him. In spite of that, I still remained firm in my position. I told him that even though his past has had a continual effect on his present, he is the only one who could make the needed changes to his life and change the trajectory of his future. When offered counseling on several occasions he declined saying, *"Yeah you right, but I'm too busy for that stuff right now."* He's told me in many ways that he wasn't willing to change nor put in the needed work to better himself. Though I genuinely loved him, I knew that I loved myself more. I loved myself enough to separate from him and all of his negative influences, even if it was to cost me a friendship and the potential of millions of dollars.

Sharing this example of Philautia Love is important to me because it came from years of hard lessons that taught me to know and value my self-worth. The old me plagued by insecurities would have succumbed to my own low self-esteem for the sake of not disappointing him as a leader. The old me would not have focused on any aspect of Philautia Love because I couldn't see beyond my insecurities. The old me had a deficiency in Philautia Love which would have forced me to lack confidence. It would have been impossible for me to have a sense of worthiness when receiving accolades based upon the hard work that I put into the success of a project. Even though the old me had to go through challenging times as well, those life's lessons made me into the man that I am today. Today, there's no monetary value that can be placed on me in lieu of my integrity, self-respect, and love that I have for myself. My love for self cannot be bought or sold. This is just one of my many examples of having enough Philautia Love. It shows how I can make the best judgment calls for myself, in spite of the opportunities around me.

Before I began studying the Greek descriptions of love, I had a very basic approach to it. I saw *Love* in its most authentic form as an innocent trusting of vulnerabilities that are expressed inwardly and outwardly through our emotions. It's not linear or one dimensional. It has many layers, facets, levels, forms, expressions and depths. The feelings of love that I have discovered for myself were built upon years of introspection, turmoil, challenges and growth. That foundation has afforded me the assurance that I matter first and foremost to myself. Because of it, I'm assured in knowing that I do not have to compromise my values or beliefs for anyone or anything. It's unfortunate to know that some people could love others more than they love themselves.

In the previous story about me loving myself more than the opportunities that were before me, I often wondered whether my former colleagues loved themselves enough to set higher standards. At times watch adults tolerate the violent verbal assaults made by him. The most they would do was shake in their boots. No one would speak up or challenge him until I joined the firm. Even then, they would not engage him directly. They would have these long sidebar conversations about how they didn't like the way he belittled them publicly. I was challenged by their need to have a polished public persona, while privately being disrespected. In his presence, they would say how much they loved him and how much he loved them. Go figure! I remember one day I got the surprise of my life when I questioned a few of them. I asked, *"Why do you take his crap?"* To my surprise, a couple of them began speaking about the monetary promises that he made to them. They were more concerned with losing the potential of earning money than the devaluation of their love for themselves. If that wasn't enough, a couple of the female employees said, *"He only talks like this whenever you're not around. That's why I appreciate your presence."* From that day forward, I couldn't for the life of me look at them or him the same. I began to ask myself the question, *"How much value do I place on my soul?"*

Though we hear and see individuals who compromise all of their worth for so little, I can't help but wonder how much they truly love themselves? What I've found out over the years is that I didn't know how to love myself either. It was because of my lack of self-love that I tolerated so much from others. That was mainly due to the measure of my brokenness, that I accepted substandard treatment from others as acceptable and normal. I accepted my brokenness as a safe place of convenience. I am not saying or suggesting that broken spirits do not love because at some point in all of our walks, we will be broken. Brokenness has three facets; either you're broken by the weight of your problems; you're broken from your bondage into freedom and rebirth; or you're still entangled in your own bondage that you need to be broken. I find it so much easier to love people from a place of wholeness versus brokenness. It is the hope that within those broken pieces that we can find that understanding and the *healing bond* that identifies where and how our breaks began. For years I was broken into many pieces. It wasn't until I received outside professional counseling that I learned *the greatest value that I can place on loving someone else is to first love myself*.

While the point of self-love is powerful, it can never be overstated. It was through 2 plus years of counseling with my psycho-therapist Dr. Shelly Neiderbach that I was forced to focus on myself. There she afforded me a safe haven to speak, cry and laugh openly about all of my failures, shortcomings and victories. It wasn't until I began to feel completely comfortable speaking honestly to her that I was finally able to put a face and name to my problems. It would take me 3 years before I understood that forgiveness of self and others was a must if I were to seek a healthier alternative to living. I had to look into the mirror and decide whether I wanted to keep functioning or begin the long process of learning how to live. Though sensitive to my needs, she reassured me that I would be just fine as she accompanied me through my emotional journey of discovering myself. It's been nearly 30 years since being in professional counseling that I have chosen to write about my understanding of love.

One of the methods that she used to discover the origins of my pain of self-hatred was to study my DNA. What she told me was that everything has a base from which it originates. She said that pain and trauma just do not start out of the sky. She began to ask me about my childhood and the many relationships that I had over the years. The longer she and I spoke about my childhood, I became more and more confused. Originally, I didn't see how my childhood had anything to do with the adult that I had become. What I eventually realized with her help, was that I was laden with invisible wounds from childhood traumatic experiences that needed to be healed. So, as I began writing this chapter on Love, I had to dig deep within myself and try to trace my initial introduction to love.

It's impossible for me to remember when the child in me met love. What I cannot say is that I knew what it was all of my life. Infants emotions are not fully developed and they have limited abilities to process emotions effectively. What I've come to believe is that most of us are born out of the Greek love of Eros. Eros is the Greek God of Love, Lust and Desires. Eros Love is often the preexisting factor when the natural process of development occurs. When 2 adults desire and lust for one another, it is peaked when they explore a more intimate physical way of expression. It is then that the egg and sperm become an embryo. This does not mean that embryos can process or understand love. What it means is that the process of development between the mother and the man that she lies with is often love.

Throughout my life, I've watched many friends as they went through the process of pregnancy. Often, I would see how their maternal instincts developed once they found out that they were pregnant. Even if they were only 2 months pregnant, I watched as they became very conscious of the areas around their stomachs. In addition to becoming more guarded, they would at times begin to establish a gentle, slow, wide, deliberate gait in their strides. It was obvious to me that they were protecting and preparing the bread that was baking in their ovens.

Upon one of my friend's infant's arrival into the world, she said that it was by far her greatest expression of joy. The Greeks describe this as Storge Love because it's the love that a parent has for their offspring. In addition, it's also rooted in unity and family. When I asked a couple more friends about how they felt emotionally once they saw their newborns for the first time, their responses were mostly centered on love. One of them even said that once the baby was delivered, she cried. I then asked why? She said that she was so amazed that she was able to bring an innocent living human being into this world. I define her birthing experience as *Innate Love* because of the natural inheritance of the deepest emotion that is a shared bond between a mother and her newborn.

In spite of the circumstances that a child enters this world, they are innocent. They do not have biases or prejudices. It's the adult guardians and parents that create the footprint by which the child will develop their biases. Babies enter into this world blindly trusting their parents, similar to those of faith who blindly trust in a higher power for guidance. In this example, trust is seen as the prerequisite to love because it's what a baby learns before they understand love. I based my perspective on an infant whose needs are being met by their parent. An infant doesn't ask for food, protection or shelter. They assume that their parent or guardian will provide it. *I will not be cold or discomforted. I cry because I'm discomforted. I am hungry. I get your attention when I cry. You will feed me because I'm crying.* In their expectation, trust becomes the assumed posture for that child. *I will not be harmed.* This trust that the child has is innate. They are born to trust until shown otherwise as they mature. Once this innocence of trust is violated, they are forced to seek other ways to find comfort in meeting their needs. Therefore, it's impossible for me to say that the infant loves their parent. To the contrary, what I can say is that trust is the preexisting factor to love for infants.

Recently I engaged a friend on the subject of love. I didn't break down the question on any of the Greek theories. I wanted to hear an honest perspective even if it differed from mine. I questioned him on whether or not trust was a prerequisite to love. Without any thought, he immediately said that it wasn't. He explained that you can love someone who you may not trust. I then asked him to elaborate on why he felt that trust was not a requirement to love. He reinforced his position by stating *"I don't necessarily have to trust the person that I love. Love is a lifestyle and it should be a way of life. It's beyond a feeling. If love was your lifestyle, then everyone would fall under the category of being loved, and trust wouldn't be a factor."* His immediate response showed me just how broad and subjective love is to each of us. You could experience it in one way while someone else experiences it in a totally different manner.

I wanted to know more about my friend's perspective on love, I asked if he could love the person who intentionally causes harm to his mother? He immediately said *"NO!"* I began to challenge him on why his position changed considering his holistic approach to love. He resigned in his position of how his loved ones were off limits. *"I can't say that I love anyone who causes harm to one of them."* His response did not surprise me. I assumed that he would answer the question on love and trust in the manner in which he did. He's like most of us who will experience love throughout our life's journey. *The longer we live and experience life, the more we will choose to love others or not.* His position reinforces the fact that there is no right or wrong answer on the definition of love and trust, and what it means to you. The interesting thing that I found is when *Love and Trust* are aligned; they are powerful emotions that yield the most rewarding results.

While the Greek description of love does not identify the foundation from an infant's perspective, I believe that trust and discipline must also be significant parts of the discussion. In this chapter on Love, trust is only one of the important ingredients that is needed in order to have sustainability with love. Another key ingredient that is essential for love when dealing with relationships is discipline. Discipline is not only relegated to the work place, intimate relationships or when dealing solely with children. It's a way of establishing boundaries. Discipline and love work hand in hand when it comes to the rearing of children. By definition, *it is the practice of training people to obey rules or a code of behavior, using punishment to correct disobedience.* There have been so many negative connotations associated with the word discipline that whenever you hear it, you automatically think that something is bad and not often enough does one associate it with good.

It was through discipline that I came to understand the depth of my parents' love for me. It was my parents who first introduced me to love through discipline. They wanted me to do all of the right things, despite the many errors of my ways. I'm sure their intentions when disciplining me and my siblings were pure and done out of love. Even though the origin of their chosen method of discipline was born out of hatred, control, and pain, they loved us. I'm sure that they did not take into account that their methodology had a long negative history that was rooted in slavery. They were only mimicking the tactics that their parents inflicted upon them; as did the slave master inflicted upon our ancestors. Let's just consider the origins of whooping with belts, sticks, twigs, etc. They are all rooted out of evil, ignorance, and pain. Though today we have a better understanding of our parents historic methodology with discipline, it does not take away from the damages that those methods of discipline had on us.

In spite of that, it's important that I speak life to a discipline that is rooted in one's interpretation of love. The use of physical force when disciplining one's children was commonly used as an acceptable method practiced within the African American community. Many have gone as far to use the Bible as a tool to justify their ways of discipline. Much of their justification with love and discipline can be found within the scriptures of the Bible. Many preachers would wait for Sunday mornings to sermonize the patrons with scriptures that support love through discipline. One of the most common scriptures used to support love through discipline can be found in the book of Hebrews 12:5-7. There, the interpretation is explained through the Son of God. *"My son, do not make light of the Lord's discipline, and do not lose heart when he rebukes you, 6. Because the Lord disciplines the one he loves, and he chastens everyone he accepts as his son. 7. Endure hardship as discipline; God is treating you as his children..."* You can also look in the book of Proverbs 13:24 *"Whosoever spares the rod hates their children, but the one who loves their children is careful to discipline them."* In these scriptures, God's discipline for his children is based out of love, but the key word in the Book of Proverbs is *"careful."*

My earliest experiences of love through discipline came through my parents. I'm not sure if at the age of 8 I truly understood what love meant. I remember my parent's lectures after every disciplinary session. They would say that they whooped me because they loved me. While that may have been their claim, it sure wasn't my experience. For the longest, I could never understand how they correlated their love for me through violence. Now please understand that my use of the word *violence* does not mean that they recklessly beat me up. I've chosen to use that phrase because of what today's studies have shown as it pertains to the use of physical force when disciplining your children.

Today's studies show that physical discipline reinforces the premise that violence is an acceptable alternative to solving problems. If through rebuking, chastising, enduring hardship, and using a rod to the backside of your child are biblical methods in which God has shown love for his children, then this study contradicts it in every way. Many of the elders from my parents' generation thought otherwise. Their generation repeated inappropriate learned behaviors that they witnessed from their childhood. It's like cyclical poverty; it's passed down from one generation to the next. In their minds based on their upbringing, physical discipline was an extension of their love for their children. They believed that their discipline was based in love and that it would dissuade the child from repeating bad behaviors. Therefore, the 8-year-old boy who lived within me will likely interpret his parent's methods of discipline as their extension of love for him; and if not corrected, he will likely pass it on to the next generation. Here it is: *They whooped me because they said that's what their parents did to them; and that's how they showed they loved me. Therefore, I am loved.*

It would take some time before I would realize that my parents discipline was a byproduct of love; in spite of the poor foundation by which certain types of their disciplining techniques were built upon. Their love for my brothers, sisters, and I exceeded the pain given from each whooping. Their discipline was deeply rooted in the pure love that they had for our success in life. They just wanted the best for us. They even extended permission to other senior family members, elementary school teachers and neighbors to discipline us. Everyone took a part in the development of my understanding of love through discipline. Separately and together our senior family members and teachers became our parents away from home. When I was a child, it was our teachers who exercised their rights to discipline us whenever we were disrespectful in school. I remember one day playing with one of my friends after we were instructed by the teacher to stop playing and sit quietly. When she got tired of verbally reprimanding us, she decided to slap our hands with her wooden ruler. If discipline was done under the context that my parents instructed, and if it was done as a quick response to alter bad behavior, then I must surmise that their discipline was also done out of love.

Our neighbors also disciplined us. Back then, our neighbors became our parents whenever they were absent. They loved us as if we were their own. It was common for me to spend the evening at one of my friend's home so that we could have continued play. We ate dinner at their tables and slept in the same beds with their children. They didn't wait to get our parents' permission. They took the reins and exercised their rights as our surrogate parents to love and discipline us. There was an understanding that discipline was an extension of love, and that was the way of life in our tightly knit community. I'm grateful today for having gone through the processes of love through discipline, even if back then I didn't completely understand my parents' delivery.

My parents displayed love through their actions. They were not the sentimental couple who adored the other's presence. To be honest, I can only recall a couple of times in which I actually saw them kiss. Though they did not often display affection before us, they made it a point to teach us love through the value of service. It was this imprint of service that was engraved in my heart at the age of 8. Whenever my siblings and I would outgrow our clothes, our parents would have us bag them up and neatly pack them in huge hefty bags. We would go to different folks' homes who would become the new recipients of our old garments. They would also take us to the homes of senior citizens to help put up the groceries; take out their garbage; and anything else that they needed done. The feelings that I began to receive as a result of giving; especially when I would see the smiles on the faces of the recipients, made me feel good on the inside. It was that feeling of satisfaction that I believe has lasted throughout my life's journey into adulthood. It is also those feelings of satisfaction that I began to identify as the love that I've been chasing.

My chasing love didn't mean that I did not have it or was looking for it in a relationship. It was more the feeling of warmth that I received internally whenever I would give of myself to another. I realized that after a while, things for me began to change. I started having euphoric sensations throughout my body. While not fully understanding these rushed feelings, I noticed that my body began going through chaotic changes due to my hormones and puberty. I wanted to share these feelings with someone else. By the time I turned 14 years old, my voice got a few octaves deeper. My underarm and groin sweat developed into an all-out musk. I started getting pimples and bumps all over my cheeks and forehead. Peach fuzz began growing above my upper lip. I no longer saw girls as girls. I saw them as young ladies with butts and boobs. Before long, I, along with my family members and close friends realized that I was growing up. I felt good knowing that I was becoming a young man.

Also, during that time in my life, I was struggling with loving the person I was. I was dealing with my own demons of lack of self-worth and rapid impulses of self-devaluation. It wasn't bad enough that the person that I saw in the mirror was ugly and full of insecurities. My problems began to mount as I entered high school as a homeless teen. Due to a traumatic fire that occurred one month prior to entering high school, we lost 2 of our close family friends who lived in the apartment below us, as well as all of our earthly possessions. If that wasn't enough, my family was forever separated.

The Red Cross and Salvation Army assisted us as we took up residence in a local welfare motel. Though weeks seemed like months and months like years, we were displaced for 2 years. My parents slept on the couch in one of my aunt's living room. My knee brother and I took up shelter in my Uncle's home before settling in the attic of another aunt's house with her dog, squirrels, and spiders. My sisters stayed in the living room of another one of my mom's sister's apartment; while my eldest brother moved in with one of my mom's brothers. I'm not complaining because most of our family and friends who supported us during this crisis showed us unconditional love. It was their love that I held on to during some of my lowest moments. Their love made me smile, laugh and feel a sense of belonging even though I didn't feel it within. Despite their willingness to give me their all, it just wasn't enough. Internally, I was a deeply troubled adolescent smiling through life's pain. I should have been in treatment or some type of counseling. It's unfortunate that we don't view psychiatric and psychological counseling as something positive. Instead, we honorably carry our heirlooms of post-traumatic stress for years, then pass it on to the next generation of innocent children.

Needless to say, I entered high school insecure, angry, and smelling like smoke. I wore borrowed clothes from family members and friends. I became very defensive because I hadn't discovered my true beauty. I didn't have a true understanding of my beauty because I spent most of my time consumed in the thoughts of what others may have thought about me, and less of what I thought about myself. I remember being late for the first day of school. I walked into a filled classroom with one vacant seat. I slowly sat down, only to be warned by the two students sitting on both sides. *"That seat is taken"* was one of their notices to me. As I looked to my left and then to my right, I felt the presence of someone standing over me. Before I could look up to acknowledge the person he uttered, *"You're sitting in my seat."* My only response was, *"it's mine now."* Feeling the need to be firm would become my posture for the 1st year of high school. I was an angry young man who was willing to share his pain.

In spite of this tough independent exterior that I displayed, I was just a lonely self-conscious boy yearning for love and attention. I only wanted to be a part of someone or something that I could love and feel good about. I needed love. That experience of meeting someone who would make me feel good about myself came quickly. One day while I was running between the bells to my next class, I ran into this young lady whose beauty stopped me in my tracks. Back then, I didn't know how to rap to a *sista*. I didn't have the skills or confidence that my older brothers possessed. I was only interested in hanging with my neighborhood friends, practicing martial arts, and throwing a football. Back then, girls were not part of my equation.

As I turned the corner, there she was standing at her locker. For the first time in my life, I met a girl who made my heart flutter. I'm not sure if she knew who I was. The only thing that she probably could say about me was, *that's the guy who always stares at me.* In any case, it didn't matter to me. The only thing that I knew was that I was in love. It was an indescribable feeling. It took everything in me to muster up the nerve to tell her *"Hi, my name is William Michael Barbee and I'm shot out over you!"* Without missing a beat, I took off endlessly running through the halls until I found shelter in a dark corner of the school's basement. I didn't know where I was going because I didn't have a destination in mind. Once I was nestled in this dark space, I began to wonder, *what in the world did I just do?* Inside of me were all of these wild uncontrolled emotions that kept me thinking about her. Later that day I told an older friend about my experience with the young lady. After taking a few minutes to laugh at me, he told me *"You're in love and you need to balance all of that energy you have."* My understanding of what he said inspired me to join the school's track team. Go figure!

Being in love became my new motto. I really couldn't explain the feeling. I only knew that I wanted to be in that young lady's presence. It was nothing for me to tell my boys that she was my girl. For the first time in my life, I had a sense of pride for something, someone that I could call my own. She was the most beautiful thing that I had ever seen. I used to stare at her European nose and huge light brown eyes. She had endless lengths of long dark brown hair that she often wore in a ponytail. She was athletic. I loved that part about her. She wasn't so caught up into her beauty that she didn't mind getting dirty. She wasn't just beautiful. She was smart and gifted and could sing the best of them under a chair. She led a song *"Pass Me Not Oh Gentle Savior"* in the school's gospel chorus. That song and her voice still rings in my heart today. I will never forget her.

Though I was smitten by this young lady's beauty, I would soon learn that being in love can also be so confusing. Psychologist Carl E. Pickhardt PhD says," When *teenagers fall in love that they're entering into a depth of caring more complex and compelling than they have known before."* He went further to make a distinction between men and women regarding falling in love. Pickhardt says, *"Often young men seem to fall in-love harder perhaps because they are more starved for emotional intimacy than young women who often have enjoyed it with close female friends over the growing up years."* I began to push aside other relationships just to be with her. I developed what Pickhardt suggested regarding that desperate attachment to her whereas *"the joy of having each other is coupled with the fear of losing each other."* Often after school I would walk with her to the bus stop, even though we lived in different areas of the city. Some nights I would catch the bus to her home once I got off from working my part-time job at a local clothing store downtown Newark. Periodically on the weekend, either my dad or sister would drop me off at her home so that we could sit and laugh with her family. I was truly smitten by her. This love relationship would last for most of my high school experience.

With this love thing being a new experience for me, I wasn't prepared for the intimacy that came with it. Prior to me kissing her, I had never kissed another woman before in my life. She was my first voluntary experience of any form of intimacy that I had with a woman. When I refer to intimacy, I'm not speaking about sexual intercourse because during the 3.5 years of dating her, we never had sex. That is one thing that I'm proud of. The intimacy that I'm referring to is the affectionate touching, holding, grinding and kissing, the things that kids do. Today, she and I occasionally laugh whenever we speak about our childhood experiences of kissing and touching. I remember one day she told me that she didn't like the way I kissed. I couldn't help but laugh because that was the first of things on my list that I didn't like about her. It was in that light moment of me hearing her utter those sentiments that my heart began to smile again.

In spite of how she felt about me, it never interfered with the love that I had for her. I was grateful for those experiences that she and I shared in our first love relationship because it better prepared me for the next one. By the time I walked into my next relationship, I had a better understanding of how to love someone with my brokenness. Brokenness was the place where I first learned to love a woman. It wasn't my destination. It was just one of the stops along my journey in life. In fact, in the first 3 months of that next relationship, I gave her my representative. I shielded her from seeing the weak and frightened little boy who lived inside of me. It was my alter-ego representative who showered her with his intellect, jokes, gifts, and laughter. I felt if that met her needs, then everything was okay. I quickly realized that I didn't have to do much more to please her. It would take me a while before I would retire my rep and put down all of my shields.

Something within me knew that this woman was the one. There was nothing that I wouldn't do for her or that she wouldn't do for me. She and I began to explore life together. Whenever you saw one of us, the other wasn't too far behind. She made a safe haven within our relationship where I was able to express myself freely and without feeling judged. She showed me how I could be loved just for whom I was. Her reciprocation of love began to show me that my staged performances of happiness were no longer necessary. What I eventually realized was that it only mattered to me that I lived in a one-bedroom attic apartment with 5 other adults. It only mattered to me that I wore my older brothers and sisters worn out clothes to work, school and church. It only mattered to me that I was dark skinned with nappy, kinky hair.

In spite of how I saw myself, she found beauty in me. The amazing thing about those naps and kinks was that she found happiness combing through them. She would kiss me on my forehead repeatedly and then begin to comb through my naps so that she could braid my shag into a *TWA - teenie weenie afro*. Her only concern was that I was happy. Her constant examples of unconditional love were like ointment to my open wounds of self-hatred, mistrust and insecurities. It was in this relationship that I was taught how love and trust felt.

Even though my maturity level could not appreciate her at the time, I continued to mask my emotions to meet her needs. That's not to say that I didn't love her or that the majority of our relationship wasn't good. To the contrary, we had a great relationship. I was in love with her and she was in love with me, despite the way in which we parted. The demise of the relationship was mainly fueled by me because I wasn't in love with myself. I lived in my lies of happiness throughout a portion of the time that she and I were together. I mastered the art of masking my feelings so that I could give her what I thought she wanted. Though she truly cared for me, I couldn't find the trust and love that I needed within myself to love her back; especially in the manner in which she deserved. I repeatedly found myself on the edge of depression after depression without knowing how to breathe. I was suffocating, dying a slow death before her eyes; and she had not a clue. What I've learned from that relationship is that it's not impossible to be loved during your brokenness, because that's what she did. She loved me from where she was and from what she knew of me. I, on the other hand, learned how to love her from the broken pieces of my shattered dreams.

In spite of all of her efforts and the love that she gave me, I left. I ran endlessly chasing after everything that resembled a piece of her love. I was trying to find happiness and love within, but I didn't know where to start. There were no directions or anything telling me to make a left at the next road and avoid the hazardous bumps. It would be me to hit every bump along the way. I hated myself for the longest time afterwards. I sought refuge in religion and church with hopes that I would get some direction. However, most of what I witnessed there was even more chaotic, hypocritical, and confusing than that of which I was experiencing on my own. I found that the closer I got to this concept of love through God in church, the more turned off I became. What was often practiced, differed from the instructions that were preached on Sunday mornings. *Do as I say and not as I do*. That truly bothered me.

As a child, church, religion, and spirituality appeared to be all in one. I struggled with connecting with my spirituality because I wrestled with the church's ideology. Often their set standards were so extreme that I and others became more focused on how we looked and less on how we felt. That was mainly due to our lack of knowledge and understanding of the biblical doctrines that we held in high esteem. The more I began to study the Bible, the more I realized how limited some of the teachings were. I began to develop a distain for the church, especially when my concerns were not addressed. There, I was told to believe that God is love. I couldn't understand for the life in me that if God is love, then why am I suffering? On the outside, I appeared to be a fine young man while my insides were bubbling over with my own low self-esteem issues. I didn't think I was worth much of anything.

I thought that church would be a viable option in helping me find love. Once I started attending services for myself, it seemed to me that the church was entrapped in its own lies, while masking the truth behind religious standards. Those standards gave many of the old guard a false sense of superiority, making them appear as though they had a chip on their shoulders. Many in the church movement felt they were entitled to this heaven, but others whose faith standards differed were heading to their own damnation. Some of those standards bearers judged others on whether or not they wore makeup, colored their hair, smoked, danced, laughed, etc. This drove me crazy. I ran into so many folks hating, back stabbing, downing, short changing, and not supporting one another. It seemed as if everyone was just going through the weekly motions of church. I thought that too many of them were missing the basic practice of extending forgiveness and love to one another.

Many times, while in service, I would just quietly watch the members as they did their praise and worship of this *God thing*. I wasn't too sure if what they were displaying was what I was in need of. I still wanted so badly to experience this Love of God that I joined the fellowship and began going through the same rituals. I would do as I saw the others do. During the altar calls, the Elders would assemble around me shouting and screaming out *"Jesus, Jesus, Jesus!"* They never asked me what I was going through. I couldn't understand why they were filled with so many emotions. Often they would grab and lift up my arms while spouting lines of *"Jesus! Yes! Praise him! Yes!"* I didn't know why they did that. Maybe they were just repeating what was done to them. The only thing that I would do is cry. It seemed that the more I cried, their yelling turned into a praise, as if I finally had my breakthrough. The only refreshing thing about that was their yelling eventually ended. I didn't know why I cried, but the posture would last for the next 20 minutes until I either had enough or the musician decided to change the melody. In their attempt to lead me to their God of Love, they failed. They scared me. I started having fears of never going back to the altar. The altar's symbolism began to lose merit and momentum. It seemed as though every action was built upon what someone heard or saw; and less on why it was instituted in the first place.

Back then, I was a church usher. It was my job to assist the basic church needs, keep a sense of order, as well as greet folks as they entered and exited the sanctuary. I remember one day when a parishioner's car alarm was sounding. I went into the parking lot to address the issue. As the alarm's sound would end, I found myself standing in a full parking lot scared. I was standing there listening to this horrible wailing sound coming from the church building's sanctuary. What I heard was nothing that I ever wanted to be a part of. That became my first look at how others may view us. It scared me. I started to just leave from the parking lot and go home, but I couldn't because I still had the church's fans and offering envelopes in my hands. Upon returning inside the church, a couple of the parishioners were at the altar giving their personal testimonies of deliverance and how happy they were. Most of their stories were horrifying. They spoke one after the other about the many tragedies that they appeared to hold up with pride. Very few, if any spoke about a goodness that was based in love.

I began to wonder why I couldn't feel the love from this God while I was there. Maybe I was spending too much time watching everyone else and less time focused on my own needs. I was just trying to fit in and be a part of something that I thought was good. The more I tried, the more baffled I became. Going to church began to confuse me even more. One part of me loved going and spending time with family and friends. Another part of me was in dire need to experience God's love, forgiveness, and wholeness of self. What I realized was that most of us were battling something in our own personal lives. Whether it was this sister over here whose son got shot; or the other one who was diagnosed with a terminal illness; or maybe the brother who is the sole provider for his family of 7 and got laid off from his job after working there for 15 years; we all have something going on.

I found that church was no longer meeting my needs. I began to see religion as a car dealership. For me it's hard to be sold a car when all of the vehicles on the lot are in disrepair. In short, I was like a car in the dealership. I was in perfect physical condition; emotionally broken with a bad transmission, engine troubles; and spiritually dead without a warranty because I hadn't a clue who God was to me. That's how I started seeing religion as a bootlegged dealership. Needless to say, I never met God in the church. I met God/ YHWH/ Jehovah/ Elohim in a hospital bed as I cried staring endlessly at the bare walls. It was in that meeting that I had the fight of my life because my twisted mind kept me believing that I could meet this God of Love and Peace by choosing death.

Most of my life was spent functioning and less on how to live. I didn't know at the time that I was battling a severe case of depression. It would take years before I would understand that my bouts with depression were my blockages that prohibited me from embracing a true sense of love of self. I started hating everything and everyone, including myself. I was sick and tired of masking my fears, insecurities, and doubts just to meet other's needs. I was tired of being the people pleaser that everyone could count on, while no one was there for me. I just wanted peace. I found fault in the littlest things. I blamed the world for all of my troubles. Never once did I stop in my tracks and have honest conversations with the man in my mirror. I became very cynical when it came to God, church and religion.

I would talk about how everyone wanted to go to this heaven but no one was willing to die. Even now when I think about it, I shake my head. Since I felt that way, I was determined not to be a coward any longer. For me at the time, the best way to see this God was to take things into my own hands. I finally reached the point where I wanted to end this madness of life. I wanted to die.

I was angry at God and disappointed in myself that I was still alive. I hated him with all that was in me. Why couldn't I just die? As I laid in the hospital bed, my mentor pulled strings with his colleagues and sought to get me immediate professional help. Though there was a no visitation policy in effect, two days later, I was surprised by one visitor. It was my father. He was the last person that I ever wanted to see. Before I got help with my issues, it was he who I blamed for a large part of my pain. He stood there and cried. I tried to remain stone face, but the power of the emotions that were present forced me to tear. I was embarrassed on many levels. The first being, I felt that I let people down who admired me. I had to face the realities of my choices alone. I was forced to accept the fact that we all are on borrowed time and this temple of a body doesn't belong to me. I always thought that I had the ultimate choice in when, where, or how I would see God since he never came to see me. What I had to learn for myself was that I had to hit my rock bottom and be broken in my spirit of doubting his existence. That's when God first revealed his spirit to me. He confronted me without judgment in the place where I resided; dead and broken. His presence gave me breath and revived my dead spirit.

Secondly, he convicted me for all of my wrongs. Though embarrassed by the choices that I made, I had to face my pain head on. No longer did I devalue life, but instead I appreciated God for sustaining the very thing that I tried to end. I was convicted and convinced that I was a servant of the Most High. During my time of solace, I only wanted to please Him. No longer did I hate myself. I began to hate sin. I began remembering Psalms 5 where it reads how *evil cannot dwell with the Father*. I began to have hope that I was forgiven by our God, the Father's grace. In that same chapter in the Book of Psalms, the last two verses read: *11 But let all those that put their trust in thee rejoice; let them ever shout for joy, because thou defendest them; let them also that love thy name be joyful in thee. 12 For thou, Lord, wilt bless the righteous; with favour wilt thou compass him as with a shield*. I knew from that point that I had another opportunity to please the Lord and that he would never leave me.

Finally, at 23 years old, God converted me from my darkness into His light. I accepted the fact that I was a sinner. I asked Him to forgive me and He granted me peace. I then accepted the fact that (Jesus) Yeshua, The Christ is the son of the living God and that He died for my sins and rose again; so that my sins will be forgiven and that I might have everlasting life. I promised Him that I shall follow His teaching from that day forward. Finally, I was born again. Had it not been for God allowing me to go through all of my troubles, I would not have come into the fullness of His love and glory. I wouldn't be here to tell you about His saving grace and that He cares. What I further realized was that God was always there. The reason why I couldn't see Him was because I was so caught up in myself. I didn't give room for having failures and shortcomings. I had to learn how to forgive myself and then others.

Though I accepted Christ as my personal savior, my body and mind had to catch up. I had to go through 2 more years of additional psychological counseling in order for me to learn how to forgive and love myself. In spite of my acceptance of Christ, I still struggled with my low self-worth and self-devaluation. My psychologist Shelly Neiderbach afforded me with tools that the church could not offer me at the time. The church was still battling with its own stigmas that they had against mental illness. Whatever the Pastor and Ministers couldn't pray out of you, it was labeled as the devil. As a fragile spirit, it was hard for me to believe that the devil lived in me and that I had no hope. I started telling folks that while God saved my soul, it was my counselor who saved my mind.

As a product of the social media generation, I find myself using all social media platforms to spread the message of love. Through organizations as the Mental Health Association of Essex and Morris County, whose mantra is "Mental illness is real. Recovery is possible," I'm able to give another face to mental illness. Through this organization, I'm able to join a team of Advocates, Consumers, and Mental Health Professionals who are committed to educating society while eradicating the stigmas associated with mental illness. I'm passionate about this path of my journey because had the stigmas not been present in my childhood, maybe years ago I would have had help for my psychological challenges. It was in my struggles with my mental health and wellness that I realized that my inability to express and experience the purest form of love, was in part due to the stigmas caused by ignorance and fear. It was also due to my inability to recognize how to value, respect and love myself. I allowed myself to be burdened by so many other issues of brokenness that it would forbid me from recognizing the love that existed within me.

I'm reminded that my story is no different than many of yours. You too had to be broken in order to be healed. You too had to learn how to get out of your own way and *trust in the Lord with all of your heart and lean not unto your own understanding.* How many times have you felt dead or abandoned by Christ? You felt as if He left you to fight your battles alone. Just yesterday I was witnessing to a mother of three who lost her main source of income. She kept telling me that every time she takes one step forward, life pulls her back two more. She said *"Where is God when I need him?"* It was painful for me to hear her because her story was too close to mine. She reminded me of myself some 28 years ago when I asked the same questions. I began to tell her that He never leaves us abandoned or dead. In fact, He will give life to those who are dead in their spirit and comfort to their aching heart. I reminded her that she was like a beautiful flower that changes with the seasons. In the fall, the trees shed their leaves as the flowers seem to die. Then we await the warmth of spring and the nourishment from the sun and rain before we begin to blossom. I encouraged her to remain steadfast and unmovable despite her doubts because her season of doubts will pass. Within a couple of weeks of her placing that call to me, she was blessed with another job. I was pleased to hear her say that her season has changed.

The same analogy that I gave her, I exercise it in my walk. Whenever I cycle on my bike, I record myself speaking positive affirmations into the atmosphere. They are not directed to any one person, but you never know who needs to hear that they are loved. That is part of the technique that I use for encouraging myself. I have to remind myself that I am loved and that it begins within me. Many of the messages that I share through social media range from perseverance to self-worth. In all, they're only reminders that I am able to push through those darkest moments. What I quickly came to realize was that there are many folks out there who follow me who have for many years suffered in silence with many of the same issues that I've struggled with. Through their direct messaging, phone calls, and even at times scheduled visits to my office, many who ordinarily would not have shared their personal stories with anyone, reach out to me for support. That's why it's become so important for me to be transparent about love and my mental health and wellness. It is my hope that somewhere someone is inspired to seek help if they're feeling lonely and unloved. You are loved!

LOVE

If you

Succeed at

Loving

Imperfect

People, then

It becomes

Plausible that

Somebody

Could love

Imperfect

You.

Bishop T.D. Jakes

UNPACKING ONE ITEM AT A TIME

CHAPTER 2

A LETTER TO HIM

MICKEY BOY

In the first book that I authored entitled *"Clipped Wings They Do Fly,"* I referenced psychologist John Bradshaw. I came to know him through a few segments of the Oprah Winfrey Show while surfing the stations. My attention was drawn by this middle aged white man speaking to an audience of predominantly women, who were all in tears. I became curious to know what he was sharing with them. At the time, I was in the midst of my own battles of low self-worth. I had contemplated suicide a number of times, but somehow on that day I did not have the courage. I didn't know anything about depression. All that I knew was that I hated the person I was. I hated myself because I was heavily weighted with my own burdens of insecurities and couldn't recognize love. I felt like I was a burden to myself. I was in my own way. It felt as if I was on fire, burning from the inside out. It was a deep dark burning of my soul. Something within me was crying out to be free.

Back then, I knew nothing about saving myself. I could not get a grip on my constant feelings of sadness and loneliness. Unfortunately, I like most folks was a pro at the craft of masking my pain away. I would skillfully use the masking technique of happiness, as I laughed and smiled through my years of tears just to get by. Yes, I was just functioning. I never learned how to live. I wrote letters and poems one after the other as if I had a captive audience awaiting me. I didn't realize that those same letters and poems would later become the impetus of my healing. Little did I know that they would become the catalyst for my first novel.

For a little over 2 years, I ended up in psychological counseling with forensic psychotherapist, Shelly Neiderbach PhD, because I was thought to be unstable. To date, I never accepted or saw myself as unstable. I learned that there was a little boy who lived inside of me, whose voice was never heard. One of the healing techniques that I learned while in counseling was how to speak to self. It was a combination of Dr. Shelly Neiderbach's theory of *"Invisible Wounds"* and Dr. John Bradhaw's *"Infancy Theory."* A combination of both of their techniques led me to my road of freedom. I would ask Dr. Shelly things about Dr. John's techniques of healing. She would skillfully weave me through a maze of intellectual theories, entangling my mind with curiosity, confusion and then hope. She told me about these wounds that I had that were not visible to the naked eye. On the onset of counseling, though she listened to everything that I had to say, I was a little confused by her approach. I thought that she was crazy. My mindset at that time was, *"What wounds?"*

As time went on, I began asking her about John Bradshaw's approach with his "Infancy Theory." I was just very curious to know if their approaches were similar. She never directly explained their similarities. However, what she offered me was that the young man I am today, has scars from his childhood. She continued telling me that every incident in my life left residuals of each encounter that I faced. She even told me that through my family lineage, the residue of slavery was somewhat engraved in my DNA. She didn't say that to mean that my physiology has strands of slavery DNA. She elaborated about the generational atrocities of slavery and how the Jim Crow Laws affected my ancestors who didn't have an outlet to express their resentment, degradation, and pains openly. She said that the good, as well as those bad experiences were embedded footprints in my mind; and if I was to heal from my past, I had to be willing to accept the past for what it was.

The longer Dr. Shelly worked with me, I eventually realized what she and Bradshaw were speaking about. There lived a little hurt boy within my spirit. I had to speak to my child within, in order for me to claim a better quality present state that would enrich my future. I needed to engage in honest dialogue with this little boy named *"Mickey."* I needed to go to a quiet place, find him, and then offer him love. I needed to reassure him that I, William Michael Barbee am now capable of providing him with the comfort, protection and love that he so deserves. It was then that I decided to write him a letter; one that reassured him that he's safe and wanted.

> *Dear Mickey, please give me this opportunity to introduce myself. I am William Michael Barbee. While you may not recognize me, you must trust me when I say that I know you. Even though I've been here all of your life, I must first apologize for ignoring you. While I'm addressing you, please know that this apology is not only for you. It's the bond that is missing between us. It's about me forgiving myself so that I can be here for you. Whenever I would see you, my heart would quickly palpitate. I would get so uneasy with my emotions that I chose not to address you. In hindsight, I should have spoken to you a long time ago. Please afford me this opportunity because it's never too late to change.*
>
> *I realized a long time ago that things weren't the best for you. I should have better protected you. I'm truly sorry about that. It was like yesterday that I remember watching you sit in the corner of the room looking afraid and feeling alone. I see you my little friend. You mattered to me then, and even more so now. I too always felt overlooked; not wanted; and that I didn't matter to most. I saw your tears and felt every ounce of your pain. Even though you may not know what you truly feared or why you were afraid to speak, know that I can truly relate to you. Back then, I didn't possess the tools needed to help myself. I couldn't get out of my own way and be there for you. I was battling many years of depression, self-hatred and a low self-esteem. I was you!*

Just as you were a baby, full of hope and promise, so was I. I had the world before me, but didn't know how to live. I was stuck in my fears of loneliness, which kept love and happiness fleeting. Even though I never had biological children of my own, my businesses filled that gap for me. For over 18 consecutive years I've produced businesses with revenues that went into the millions. I thought that I had everything that I had ever wanted and needed. I had a false sense of happiness. I was crowded around many people whose needs were dependent upon my ability to produce revenue. Their dependency made me feel like I was the most important person on the planet. I tried to solve everyone's problem before addressing my own. I was a people pleaser. As shameful as it may sound, it was the truth. Let me apologize for not seeking to first please you.

In spite of all of my successes, I still battled with my own insecurities and low self-esteem. My persistent self-devaluation created complete silence in the loudest of spaces and a lot of noise in the emptiest rooms. Whenever I heard my voice, it echoed 10 times or more with a deafening audible pain. I want you to know that I feel your pain. It wasn't long before I realized that with all of those people and the millions of dollars that I had around me, so too came their problems. My world continued to spin out of control and pass me by. Every night when the lights went out and everyone went home, I was left to fend for myself. I can't say that I felt alone, but what I can say is that often I felt a sense of emptiness. Where there once existed 40 people a day, I am now left to hear the noises of their chatter creeping out of the bare walls and empty rooms that they left behind. The crowded hallways, in which they walked, are now littered with their fragmented memories; even they began to close in on me.

My feelings of emptiness got even worse after I closed down 3 of my 7 companies. It was like I had to bury my own children. No one understood me and neither was I prepared to face their deaths alone. I couldn't for the life in me go to someone and talk to them. What would I say? Who would I say it to? How do I tell someone in the urban environment, who already thought of me to be this privileged individual, that I was not happy with the direction of my life? Can I truly complain to those that I paid and signed their checks about how money ain't everything; when in fact the little I paid them barely sustained their families? So once again I felt voiceless. I quickly reverted back to self-medicating my feelings, fears and pain. For comfort and to pacify my emptiness, I started listening and trying to solve everyone's problems.

Mickey, I just want you to know that I see you over there and no longer will you be ignored. I have so much to give you. I want to welcome you into your destiny. Please know that you do have a voice; and I'm here to listen. I love you!

Mickey, you matter! Let's go home!

I had to write this letter to Mickey, letting him know that I didn't forget him and he could finally come home and rest. He was this shy, bashful, fragile little boy, who lived in the shadows of his older siblings. Due to his low self-esteem, he never fought to be recognized. He never realized his true value. For comfort, he ran and hid in the bosom of his mother. He never yearned or desired attention from anyone except her. She nicknamed him *"Mickey"* after the cartoon character *Mickey Mouse*. Often, he recalled his mother playing with him. She would hold him in her lap, and with her long fingernails, run them up his backside to his neck. He'd just fall out laughing in her arms, waiting for her to do it again.

She protected, nurtured and loved him. She was his God-send. She was the closest person to him that he could have ever imagined to be of God. She was perfect and nonjudgmental. She accepted him though he had not begun to accept himself. She was his provider and comforter of all of his needs. She was his ear during his moments of uncertainty and despair. She was his in-house counselor, there to guide him whenever he couldn't figure out his way. She sacrificed her comfort to meet his needs. Because of who she was to him, it is every reason why he cherishes each moment with her today.

Though 40+ years have passed and there are over 200lbs of body weight, I am that little boy *Mickey*, who could have never imagined getting old. In my mind, I was not destined for longevity. In fact, I was trying to make it day by day. One of the most pivotal moments that I had with my Mom came during my childhood. Though many studies show that kids do not remember events prior to the age of 4, I remember many events that date back to my tender age of 2. I would watch my brother, who is 1 year and 6 days older than me take my place in my mother's lap. My brother suffered from a severe case of asthma. Nightly, we slept with a medicated vaporizer in our bedroom to help him breathe. Whenever he had an asthma attack, Mommy would put me down and pick him up. She comforted him in her bosom on our sun porch, as he struggled to breathe. I can remember that as if it were yesterday. Even now, my emotions are getting the best of me with just the thought of how much she loved us. In spite of me being a *mama's boy* and with all of the love that she gave me, it still was not enough.

Being a *"mama's boy"* had its perks, as well as its share of burdens. That means if I'm a *"mama's boy,"* I couldn't possibly be a *"papa's boy."* It was hard for me to establish a strong relationship with my father because I was too afraid of being near him. Deep within, I believed that I represented every problem that my mom presented to him. Whether it was those nights that we were without heat, where we hovered around the kitchen stove; or his lack of maintaining a job to feed his family, due to seasonal layoffs; or even an accident that my mom had with the only family car; I felt responsible for mommy's existence which at times ignited his anger. I'm not too sure as to why I felt this way because in hindsight, he did not hold me accountable for those things. This is just how a wounded Mickey felt. When they fought, I suffered. The more he yelled, the more compromised my comfort became. Though his frustrations were directed at her, I felt her pain because it was me who sat under her. She would put me down and take the needed time to lick her emotional and psychological wounds. He ensured that his mouth and intimidation tactics would be just as painful as his physical capabilities. I clinched to my mom's thigh to anchor my fears.

This man that I came to know as my father wasn't the man that I desired to meet as an infant. I would even say that he wasn't the man that the kid Mickey wanted to deal with either. If you allow my imagination to take you on a tour of my birth, it tells me that the man that was there during my infancy had a soothing baritone voice. I would like to believe that it was through my mom's stomach walls that he sang love songs to me, calming my nerves with his voice. It was his tone that I felt a sense of comfort and protection. It reassured me that I could reach the end of my journey to infancy because he was there. Upon arrival day, I longed for the same security of his voice once I hit the birthing table weighing in at 7lbs2oz. I came out of my mother's womb with expectations of being accepted, wanted, and free. Yes, I came prepared to claim that which was mine, yeah, his voice.

I can only imagine as with most infants, I too was egocentric. I believed in only me and what I needed at the time. I wasn't driven by thoughts that there may be others with more pressing needs than my own. It was all about me until early one morning when things changed. It must have been the morning of Thursday, May 5, 1966; 7 days after entering into this world that I met this whisker filled man as he laid on his back in his bed. He lifted me high above his head, reassuring me that I would not fall. Even though I didn't know him, I totally trusted him. Slowly and gently he raised and then lowered me to his presence, where I felt the pain of his stumbled whiskers. I threw up on him and then endlessly cried. Exhausted by the noise from my crying and the filth of my vomit, he placed me on the bed next to my brother who endlessly stared at me. He looked at me as if he too could lift me up. I would be telling you a lie if I said that I remembered my *Infancy Journey*. I can only imagine what that experience must have been like. That in which I do know is that I needed to go back to a place of chronicling Mickey's journey in life, especially to the point of having an understanding of his story. I needed to experience Mickey's times of innocence. I needed Mickey to know that he was wanted, desired, planned, and loved; and not just by one of his parents, but by both of them.

When I consider my earliest memories of my father, there are many. Therefore, please forgive me if it appears as though I'm painting him out to be this monster of a man, because in all actuality he wasn't. He was kind and often generous with his words and compliments. He made the least of them feel like Kings and Queens. For those who thought they were worthy of accolades, he'd laugh and smile with them while slowly shooting them down from their self-righteous pedestals. He was a defender of the underdog, who at times didn't mind standing alone. He was known by those at his church, to be a comforter. He was a man who consoled those who were saddened and cried endlessly whenever he was giving praise and honor to his Lord and Savior. The irony with his actions was the man that I witnessed at church was different from the one who brought me there. He had a charm about him that was addictive to all he met. It was in the church where he found his calling as a Deacon; yes, a Deacon. They saw value in him. He was one of the men existing amongst the flock of desperate, angry, lonely women. There his charming skills were sharpened. From the very mouth that he used to impose fear and intimidation on me, it was now being used to pray over other's lives. I could only imagine what they saw in him.

Though my father's been deceased for 11 years, it was imperative to study his emotional DNA because it enabled me to understand who I am as a man. This idea of associating my father's past with who I am will show the lineage of why I may do things the way in which I do. One of the good things that I most remember about him was how he constantly told others how he prided himself on being a father and a provider for his family. Most of my childhood, I took offense to his pride in being the father that he was. He occasionally boasted about all of the things that he was supposed to do. It's as if he was doing us a favor by staying in the house and providing for us. At the time, I was too young to appreciate his actions because I couldn't get past my fear of him. He, along with many men of his generation were not the emotionally supportive or understanding parents to their children. For them, it was a sign of weakness whenever a man showed any form of sensitivity. Their commitment to being a provider was the extension of their love for their children and family as a whole. They prided themselves on going out and making an honest living for their families. They left the emotional needs in the hands of the mothers. Where my father failed his little son was that Mickey's needs from him were not primarily based on provisions, but instead in his inability to show him affection.

As I chronicled Mickey's journey to his place of his innocence, I realized that he was there waiting for my return. Therefore, if my father had the knowledge to reclaim the child that he left behind, he too would have been there waiting for his return. My father was the product of a handsome, debonair, athletic man who impregnated a dainty southern church girl. Back in the late 1920's, it was not fashionable for a woman to be a single parent. Upon my unwed grandmother becoming pregnant with my father in early November of 1930, she did everything in her power to lock my grandfather down. She left the city of Durham, NC and placed my father in the care of her older sister as she chased my grandfather around the country. Contrarily, my grandfather did everything in his power to get away. After impregnating a few more women, he took to the road to play in the Negro Baseball League for a division within the Baltimore Black Sox with some of his Paterson, NJ and Baltimore, Md cousins. When the playing season ended, he was employed by the railroads and became a member of the "Brotherhood of Sleeping Car Porters." I raise the issue of my grandparents, not to shame them. It's because in order for me to speak of the boy I was, I had to deal with the boy my father was.

My father had to live with the knowledge that while his parents were alive, yet absence throughout his youth, he was not their priority. He was not their foremost concern. It must have been devastating for a young boy who was raised by his relatives, to know that his parents were alive and consciously chose not to physically be in his life. This isn't to say that his aunt and uncle who raised him didn't love him. Neither does it suggest that his parents didn't love him either. This speaks to the need of the child who always lived wondering what it feels like to be completely accepted and loved by his parents.

Whenever my father would speak about his childhood, I'd listen attentively. He often spoke about how his guardian use to beat him with whips, belts, and at times his hands. He spoke as though what he experienced as a form of discipline was needed to be transferred down to the next generation of family members as some type of prized heirloom. I shook in my boots just listening in amazement of how someone could ever survive what he went through. Not only did he speak of the discipline in his home, he further spoke of the discipline outside of the house. He said that his neighbors had the rights of passage to beat him and other kids who did wrong like they were their own. For him to still reference the discipline that came from a community versus his parents, must have been confusing for him as a little boy. After his graduation from Armstrong High School in Richmond, Va., he enlisted into the United States Marine Corps where he fought in the Korean War Conflict. Even with the stories of brutality that he witnessed and was a part of, I still sat engaged to hear more. The more he spoke, the sadder I got.

Part of my sadness evolved because I'm now hearing an older man indirectly speak about the absence of his biological parents in his life. I'm sure that he experienced aspects of the *"Abandoned Child Syndrome"* as one of his major issues while growing up. Psychologist Claudia Black M.S.W., Ph.D. speaks about the feelings that children develop as a result of abandonment are displayed through feelings of toxic shame. *"You are not important. You are not of value."* She further suggests that the power of emotional abandonment often occurs *"when a child has to hide a part of who he or she is in order to be accepted, or to not be rejected."* I can vividly see the boy that my father was seeking approval for his very existence. I also believe that the other shame with my father's experiences is that he never got a chance to allow the little boy within him to live. Dr. Black explains what hiding a part of oneself means *"it is not okay to make a mistake. It is not okay to show feelings; being told the way you feel is not true. You have nothing to cry about and if you don't stop crying I will really give you something to cry about. That didn't hurt. You have nothing to be angry about."*

Even though my Dad's love for us was strong, he couldn't overcome the tragedies of his childhood. While his childhood abandonment issues may have plagued him throughout his entire life, he was still able to raise a family of 5 children and be married to one wife until his death. In spite of what was done to him, he made it his priority that we not experience his absence from our lives. He broke that cycle, the strand within our DNA patterns. We were the light in his eyes and the hope for his tomorrows. From every accomplishment, award and even in our trials, he stood in support for our victories. His willingness to speak to others about his children and grandchildren's accomplishments was never hidden. If you had the honor of knowing him, you would know that through his own personal challenges, he was still an honorable man in the eyes of those who knew him.

Once I began counseling, I got the needed professional help that would aid in my emotional and psychological liberation. Unfortunately, while in counseling, I struggled with identifying the correlation of my struggles to my father's childhood pain. Initially, I didn't understand how what happened to him could impact me. It took a little while to get it. Once I understood it for what it was, I began to see him with much pity. I felt sorry for the child that always searched outside for attention, approval, and love. I felt sorry for the child who had to deny himself and learn poor coping skills that would lead him to a path of manipulating others. I felt a sense of sadness in knowing that my father who loved, protected, and guided me into adulthood didn't have the needed support that would help him along his journey. How cool would it have been had his child within lived bold and free? I can only imagine that in death would his little boy find peace.

I also wondered about the similarities between my father's little child within and my Mickey boy. What would they say to one another? Aside from blood relations, would they be friends? What strikes me the most is how my little boy Mickey's experiences mirror the painful descriptions that Dr. Black describes, are similar to my father's adult abandonment issues from his childhood. As early as I remember, my father after whooping me and my siblings would tell us to stop crying before he gave us something to cry about. Just as he was forced to hide his true feelings of pain, sadness and loneliness; he imposed his unhealthy coping skills on us. Often people repeat the same bad behaviors that were done to them, children learn what they live. Psychotherapist Christine Langley-Obaugh reinforces that belief when she says *that "We repeat what we do not repair."* Repairing to me meant if I don't end this cycle of abuse, it will continue to live on through me.

As I continued in counseling to end my father's unresolved childhood issues that he imposed upon me; I started reading and studying stories about individuals who have experienced some of the same challenges that I've been through. In doing so, I've learned that I was not alone in my plight. What I've found to be certain is that more and more people have been on the receiving end of their parent's unresolved childhood issues. Many victims, including my parents have sat silently while trying to cope with their parent's ills. As for my parents' generation, there were no services to address their mental health issues. They truly had to fend for themselves. It became my mission to raise the consciousness of those who selfishly impose their pain on the innocent lives that they're charged to protect. I've also taken the lead on being transparent with my struggles because the more transparent I am, the more therapeutic it's been for me. It is my cry that everyone takes the needed time to liberate their children within.

It was Life Coach Iyanla Vanzant who said that *"To get where you're going, you must acknowledge where you've been."* Through my acknowledgement, I am reminded of a young, shy, sensitive Mickey who had to live under the control of his wounded father. I can better understand how trapped he may have felt. Mickey never established his own identity as long as he feared his father. Instead, he learned how to become a people pleaser in order to get by. There was nothing that he wouldn't or couldn't do. He worked from the time he was born up until now. If the laws of today were enacted when he was growing up, my father would be under the jail for violating all labor laws. I ran to his beck and call, from sun up to sun down. He would call me from different parts of our home just to pour him milk, water, or fetch him anything that he wanted that was in the refrigerator, which was only a few feet from where he was sitting. It was nothing for me, a nervous kid to spill hot and cold water or beverages on him as I was summoned to pour. I was his personal nervous waiter. No sooner than I was done with that chore, I took to the stairs in search of my brother to play with or my Mom's side to hide.

I tried my best to avoid him at all cost. He was the *"biggest and baddest"* man that I'd ever known. It would be some 20 years later that I realized that this giant of a man only stood a meager height of 5'2" tall. His presence alone made me quiver. I watched as he boldly shut grown men down, forcing them to abandon their positions. Though I marveled at his courage, I was still afraid of that threat that he would impose on me. The more that I think about it, if I had children of my own, I would not have wanted them to fear me in the manner in which I feared him. I believe that respect is earned by love, and shouldn't always have to come by fear, violence, or intimidating tactics.

It was my Dad's reputation that made things bad for me. Some relatives thought his approach to disciplining us was funny. It was nothing for me to hear insults from a relative while we were playing a board game, referencing that they were going to beat me as though they were my father. Even though everyone who was present laughed, I never found humor in it. I was more embarrassed and ashamed that his reputation for beating us went beyond the walls of our home. I always wondered if these relatives truly thought the discipline used on me was funny, then why didn't they have the courage to rescue me? Some years later, I spoke to the main relative and asked them, not about my father but instead about something that took courage for them to face. After hearing his response to my question on courage, I had a better understanding why he never came to my rescue. I asked, *"Why didn't you March on Washington or demonstrate during the Civil Rights Movement?"* Not being prepared for what he had to say, I gasped. His exact words were, *"I was a coward."* His response shocked me to say the least. I now understood my father's plight. He never had anyone to teach alternative ways of loving. I also had my own reality check of forgiveness. I had to forgive even those self-professed cowardly relatives who teased me about my father's brutal nature because of their lack of courage. Now I realize that I couldn't expect them to rescue me when they too were afraid of him.

Until his death at the age of 75, I don't believe that he ever allowed the child within him to heal from his childhood of abuse, neglect, abandonment, and brutality. By knowing his history, it helped me to understand more of who I am. It helped me to see why I process things the way I do emotionally. Often, I find myself withdrawn and afraid to speak from my heart. I can even equate some of these good and bad attributes directly to him and my mother. It's so important that I tap into my parents' historical experiences so that I can be a better me to me and then to everyone else. Therefore, it's not a surprise that Mickey experienced a world of pain at the hands of a man's arrested development. The young Mickey began developing early coping techniques so that he could survive. He learned how to smile at the drop of a dime and immediately turn away whenever he was being looked upon by his father. If truth be told, the abusive inflictions of pain that my dad imposed upon me, was due to his reality of mirroring those bad behaviors that he learned. He was no more than a product of his time and environment. I'm not coming up with an excuse for his behavior or for what he did, I'm merely stating a fact.

While this is just my opinion, it is important that I break the cycle of his issues of abandonment that have caused him not to live honest and free. Another fact is that our ancestral link to slavery and the atrocities became learned behaviors that we adapted as forms of discipline to our offspring. Throughout the years of my life, there were always staunch comparisons to the way whites disciplined their children vs. the way Blacks disciplined theirs. This is not etched in stone that all or even most families, be it white or black disciplined their children in the designated manner. It's been long laughed upon in the African American community how white folks send their kids to "time out" sessions while black families send their children to get the belt for a whooping.

To better support my perspective on my father, grandfather, and great grandfather's link to slavery, I have read many books that connect our form of discipline to slavery. There's a book entitled *"Black Rage"* that was written by Dr. William H. Grier and Dr. Price M. Cobbs where they have done research to support their position that black folks learned to beat their children from slavery. An excerpt from the book states, *"Beating in child-rearing actually has its psychological roots in slavery and even yet black parents will feel that, just as they have suffered beating as children, so it is right that their children be so treated. This kind of physical subjugation of the weak forges early in the mind of the child a link with the past and, as he learns the details of history with slavery per se."*

As a direct result of this subjugation that the children experienced, it becomes a part of their subliminal DNA. This is not to say that all or even most of the children, when they become parents will discipline their children in the same manner. What I am merely implying is that there are cyclical damages to the generations of Africans whose ancestors were enslaved during the middle passage. Harvard Medical School Psychiatrist Dr. Alvin F. Poussaint states that *"It's culturally embedded in America that spanking is a legitimate and good way to discipline children. But the fact is, nearly all studies, except for a few, say it is not a good way of disciplining and can actually produce damage."* He also said, *"We have such damage in the black community, when you add to parents beating their kids; it's sending the message that violence is an okay way to solve problems."*

I was always under the belief that the form of discipline that I received from my dad was acceptable. However, after years of therapy and counseling for my issues as an adult, there have been direct correlations to the manner I was raised. Upon my rebellion in my early 20's, I began to question how effective this form of discipline was after realizing that I was left with physical and emotional scarring to my body and mind. Was it more effective that I feared my dad, or was it more important that I respected him through love? I realized after my counseling that if I feared him, I would always try and avoid him, or seek a way to topple him through another form of disrespect. If I were to respect the manner of discipline that wasn't violent, I believe I would have benefited from the latter form of discipline without having sustained as many emotional scars.

My day of toppling my dad finally came to pass. Though at the time I didn't have a full understanding of depression, I knew that I was in crisis at the moment. For a little over 2 months my dad wouldn't speak to me. He did everything in his power to avoid saying anything to me. I knew I didn't do anything to him to make him sever communication with me. I'd walk in while he was in the midst of reading his Bible and say hello, but to no avail. I'd make a sandwich right in front of him; he would just sit there as though I mattered not. I would even come into the house from a long evening at work and try and engage him. He would still ignore me as though I was not there. It was then that I would go into my mom's bedroom where I would seek understanding. I would whisper to her about my dad who was in the next room. I didn't understand her emotional limitations that were the result of living in the same conditions that I was subjected to, I still sought understanding from her. What she offered me was comfort. She chose to address my invisible wounds that I couldn't see. In spite of her bandages, my wounds continued to leak.

It happened on a Saturday, somewhere around noon. I was headed to South Jersey to meet up with a friend who was home from college. I came home only to change my clothes when he met me at the back door. As soon as I walked in, he began to follow me around the small apartment as though he was looking for me to make a mistake. Within seconds, he got his wish. I made my first mistake. I came home! He asked me, *"What's your problem?"* With a nervous and confused look on my face, I stared at him in amazement. One part of me wanted to respond, while the wiser more experienced me chose to take my time. Before I could part my lips, his pointer finger was in my face, waving and poking me across my nose to cheeks, cheeks to nose. For the first moment or so, I stood there boiling on the inside. I heard "Mickey" screaming out to me, *"Help! Help!"* Somewhere I mustered the nerve to topple this giant of a man. Though physically I towered over him nearly 8 inches, I still feared him. He had done so much psychological damage to me that I saw him to be bigger than life.

It was my mother whose presence I would remember. Though she spent most of her time in a wheelchair, I saw her standing in the doorway just feet from my father. I'm sure she must have called out my name a few times, but I didn't remember. What I most recall was the tone of her voice. It wasn't one that I had ever recalled hearing. It was a screeching sound of alarm as I raised my fist and pushed my body against my father. I found myself in unfamiliar territory. The thought of me attacking anyone alarmed me, especially since it was my father. It was the first time in my life that I saw fear in both of my parent's eyes. In hindsight, it must have been his little boy that I caught a glimpse of, as I was about to pummel him. It must have been "Little Donny" who saw *"Mickey Boy"* for the first time. That alone frightened me. I caught myself questioning what was I doing? Watching his fear for me forced me to part from his presence as he stood there big eyed and frozen, knowing that I saw him as a vulnerable human being.

While this story may be alarming to most, it's not surprising when you think about Dr. Alvin F. Poussaint theory that beating of your children will leave subliminal imprints in their minds that violence is an acceptable way of solving problems. It had to have been the grace of God that was granted to my father on that day. I was on the verge of inflicting violence upon him just to silence the beast in him that lived in my head. Imagine if my father had the willingness to express his sentiments and feelings of loneliness and abandonment that he experienced throughout his lifetime. Imagine if he felt that it was acceptable to allow that "Little Donny" who lived inside of him to get help so that he could speak for himself. I can only wonder what he would say. Maybe he too would be crying out for help. I can even see the similarities between little Donny and Mickey because they shared in the same experiences of pain inflicted upon them by their guardians. Just imagine, if everyone would take accountability for their actions that they impose on others, imagine how life would be.

It saddens me to know that my dad and so many of us spend lifetimes masking and bottling up those little beautiful, creative, scared boys and girls who were only trying to be loved. What I have come to accept about my father is that hurting people hurt people. That is why it's imperative that we put an end to this successive poverty of our traits, behaviors and norms that are passed down from one generation to the next. We must stop looking out at our own cultural flaws as being acceptable without addressing them at their roots. Just because things are considered to be traditional, it doesn't mean that it's right and should continue. I can only wonder if there is another who is willing to write their inner child a letter? If so, tell them that you are looking forward to meeting them.

At my father's grave I said:

"Daddy, I forgive you!"

UNPACKING ONE ITEM AT A TIME

CHILDREN LEARN WHAT THEY LIVE

If a child lives with criticism, He learns to condemn.

If a child lives with hostility, He learns to fight.

If a child lives with ridicule, He learns to be shy.

If a child lives with shame, He learns to feel guilty.

If a child lives with tolerance, He learns to be patient.

If a child lives with encouragement, He learns confidence.

If a child lives with praise, he learns to appreciate.

If a child lives with fairness, He learns justice.

If a child lives with security, He learns to have faith.

If a child lives with approval, He learns to like himself.

If a child lives with acceptance and friendship,

He learns to find love in the world

Dorothy Law Nolte

UNPACKING ONE ITEM AT A TIME

CHAPTER 3

FORGIVENESS

Forgiveness is the gift that you possess that will eradicate the evils from your spirit.

Damn, that hurts! It's easier said than done. As I travel and listen to so many stories from people around the country, I find that many of us are held hostage to our past pain and bitterness. We just can't let it go. How often have you uttered the words "I forgive you," only to bring back the actions of the individual to whom you said you forgave? It's truly unfortunate that most of us will never fully forgive someone because of our own subconscious, and at times conscious needs to nurture past offenses. I totally understand how hard it is to forgive someone who has willfully wronged you. I too have been guilty of that exact thing, holding on to a piece of pain that I wasn't ready to let go.

It was pride that got in the way of my freedom. I would just sit comfortably in my seat of *"needing to be right"* that I failed to realize the opportunities that were before me of being happy and liberated from that other person's offenses. Due to my own idiosyncrasies, I never made a connection between my needing to be right over my choosing not to forgive the other person for their offenses. Far too often many of us allow our pride to block our blessings. It's as though we feel that we are compromising or losing something should we offer forgiveness to someone. Often, we become consumed with thoughts of being perceived as weak in the eyes of others should we yield to the kind acts of forgiveness. It's like clockwork. We then begin to wrestle with the *"If I"* thoughts. *What would they think if I...? How would they view me if I....?* While those may be normal responses to the rational thought process, we have to learn that it's totally okay to be vulnerable and experience those types of emotions as well. Vulnerability, when used properly is a sign of strength.

Unfortunately, many of us subconsciously find it too comforting not to allow ourselves the right to forgive. Please let it be clear that I'm not suggesting that the process of forgiveness is easy. True forgiveness can be a long and arduous process, depending on the nature and depth of the pain. Often it takes a lot of work on the offended person's behalf before they are truly able to heal. In spite of all, it is still a conscious choice that one must make if they're truly seeking it. Every time that I hear someone say that I can't forgive another person, my heart aches. I can only pray that they come to the realization that their inability to forgive the person who offended them isn't for the other person's benefit. The initial reward in the process of forgiveness is for your benefit, even if you don't feel or realize it at the time. You owe it to yourself to allow the process of healing to unfold in your journey. You must begin to exhale those negative thoughts from your mind, heart and spirit. You deserve to be free! Choosing not to free yourself from those negative emotions will only leave the door open for bitterness and spiritual damnation.

While we can have a long discussion on bitterness, I choose not to go too deep on this emotion. There is nothing that I can contribute to the discussion of bitterness that is positive. According to Dr. Stephen Diamond, bitterness is *"a chronic and pervasive state of smoldering resentment and it's one of the most destructive and toxic of human emotions."* Therefore, if you become bitter, you can never attain the freedom from the pain that you are holding on to until you decide to let it go. Bitterness leads to depression and other mental and physical illnesses that prevent an individual from achieving their full potential. As simple as it may sound, everyone has a right to feel pain, hurt and despair. Also, we have the right to experience the beauty and power of forgiveness for yourself and for others. How often have you held onto someone else's grudge only to find out that your loved one forgave the person a long time ago?

It always amazes me how we seek forgiveness daily from a God that we cannot see, but yet and still we choose not to forgive those who we see daily. This irony has to stop. It is by far one of the biggest contradictions that people make; using religion as a tool to hide their own insecurities. That same tool has been used to impose wars on nations as well as guilt and shame upon individuals. These gatekeepers of religious sects' struggle with the same human behaviors. In spite of that, the basis of most religions are built upon something powerful and good. Its basic principle is to love and forgive others. How could I love someone I'm not willing to forgive? How can I forgive someone who I'm not willing to love? Both love and forgiveness are entangled in an illicit affair. While they do not need the other in order to be substantiated, together they're a powerful force.

In spite of the relationship between love and forgiveness, it must be known that forgiveness does not constitute that one must love the one who committed the offense against them. Recently I've watched the many sexual accusations made against priests in the Catholic Church. The church has paid out tons of money to victims of sexual pedophiles who reside in the leadership in their churches. In most of those cases, there was no public admission of guilt by the church or priests who allegedly committed those atrocities. One may argue that these types of sins are first and foremost crimes; and that they are unforgivable offenses that must be punishable under the law. In spite of how you may feel about those offenses, at some point it is still the hope that the offended can arrive to a place of forgiveness for the person or act that they committed. This will free them from the pain of the vile act that was attached to the crime committed against them. Furthermore, forgiveness of the person does not mean that one must love that person who offended you. It's almost impossible to expect a victim to love the perpetrator who violated them for 30 plus years. What forgiveness offers you is a healthier alternative for healing and freeing yourself from the acts committed against you.

An example of true forgiveness and love that is dear to my heart occurred nearly 20 years ago when I lost a good friend to a senseless crime of violence. This friend's story is intertwined with many years of loving family relationships, neighborhood territorial feuds, women, and lies. I've watched firsthand how friends, who once played together as children, killed the other over an alleged relationship with a young lady. However sad this may sound, senseless violence has become a way of life in some communities across America. I was shocked to see the family of the felon teen attend the funeral services of the murdered friend. Though tensions were high, I was amazed to hear the mourning family call for peace at the funeral services. Who does that? Many of us who witnessed that were baffled. Initially I couldn't believe what I was seeing and hearing. I, along with everyone present, was humbled by the gesture. Even though there would be more retaliatory killings of others, including friends on both sides, it never stopped a deeper need to love and forgive that each of the families sought to achieve from the other.

While we all speak of the need to forgive, how many of us are truly willing to forgive someone who takes the life of someone that you love? I'm sure many of us would respond positively should we ever be polled in a public questionnaire. History has shown me that the majority of us can't even forgive a person who accidently offends us. So, having expectations that they will forgive someone for something greater would be foolish. What is obvious to me that love was the major contributor to both families. While one family may have been challenged by the lethal acts of their loved one, it did not stop the depth of love that the victim's family had for them.

What's more interesting to me about this particular story is that it reinforces the point that forgiveness is a choice that you have to want to give someone. This family did not have to forgive the murderer. They could have just stayed in their emotions and it would have been understood by everyone. So, by them choosing to forgive the murderer and not hold the family members accountable for their loss is rare. It also speaks to the value and need to seek forgiveness as a way of healing. During and after the process of bereavement, these families chose forgiveness as their first step to healing. It is because of the power of love and forgiveness that I find this story so important to discuss.

There's nothing worse than going to a grave knowing that you were not forgiven or haven't offered someone forgiveness. For a couple of years, I studied, graduated, and practiced Mortuary Science. It was in my Funeral Services and Bereavement classes that I learned that funerals are the event, while the bereavement is a process. Upon graduating, I got a job as a Funeral Director at a local funeral home. There, all of my classroom knowledge would be tested. Family members of the deceased would share good and bad stories about their loved one. What captivated my attention most was while I was making their arrangements, the method by which each person grieved was different. Some mourned and grieved openly while others internalized their feelings. In any case, there's nothing wrong with either process.

I began to get somewhat jaded by some of the stories that folks would share. I began to question myself as to whether or not I was in the right profession. I've heard everything from rape, molestation, abuse, and neglect. However, in most cases they spoke about how much they loved their deceased loved one. What also intrigued me was how some of the mourners would hold on to pain and regrets as though they were treasures. Occasionally someone would say how if they were given another opportunity to have time with the deceased, they would ask them to forgive them for some past debts. Whenever those sentiments were expressed, I noticed how different ones in the family would clam up. It was as though they were in some way embarrassed that these comments were being expressed in front of me. On the other hand, they seemed to have a sense of relief, almost affirming what was just spoken. I began to think about how nice it would be if we shared with our loved ones our willingness to forgive, love and appreciate them before they close their eyes. Hopefully then, we would not be left with the regrets of the *"would of, could of, should of"* sermons.

It is paramount that you know that you have the right to forgive others and yourselves, even if you were the one at fault. Even though you may never utter the words, *"I'm sorry, please forgive me,"* it's imperative that you find closure and offer the other person the same. Never forget, good people make mistakes too. It was in that understanding that forced my light bulb to go on. I was reminded how I was accused of hurting someone's feelings I loved dearly. It was never my intention to do so. There was nothing that I wouldn't do for that person. That's how much I loved and respected them. So, for them to be offended by my actions truly hurt my feelings. At first, I got offended by the very inference that they thought I did something negative to them that would hurt their feelings. It was only when I removed my feelings and sought to understand their perspective, that I was able to see their point of view. No, it wasn't my intent to offend them, but I did. It was then up to me after recognizing my offense that I sought forgiveness from them.

It was through many examples of offensive words and/or actions that I began to recognize the mode of my delivery differed from the expectations that others had of me. A few years ago, I reluctantly attended a church service at a small family-based Pentecostal church. I didn't hate the church or the Pastor who delivered the sermon. I just wasn't a fan of the way he preached. In spite of my lack of desire to hear what he had to say, I sat attentively listening to every word of this particular sermon. He spoke on the power of tact. In his example he highlighted the intentions of a person who was trying to feed a flock of birds. He said that when his son fed the hungry birds, they all scattered because of the method in which the seeds were delivered. He threw them at the birds. With safety as their utmost focus, the birds were forced to fly away. Bewildered by the birds rush to flight, the boy began to cry. His father comforted him and began to take the feed out of his hands and toss the same seeds to the birds that have now returned to eat.

I embraced the lesson in this sermon because it worked for me. I had to start being more conscious of my mode of delivery. I had to take in account that maybe, just maybe I was having a bad day when that person asked me for help. Even though I helped them as much as I could and probably to the best of my ability, the manner I did was perceived as offensive. I too, like the son may have had the good intentions to help, but was not conscious of the way I delivered my assistance. It would take me being humbled before I would recognize this basic principle and forever be conscious of my role in unintentional offensive behavior.

I chose to do the hard work on how to better manage my role in relationships with people. I had to get out of my own way in order to help myself. As my brother often says, *"we're bombarded with our own idiosyncrasies."* Our minds are full of trickery. We want to believe that what we see, hear, and feel is a fact. What I realized was that I never considered that the other person's experience of the same event that just occurred may have been different from mine. My intentions may have been to help them, but my actions made them feel subservient, as though I'm doing them a favor. I had to learn to breathe and step back for a moment before I allow my emotions to take control of my actions. It was in that truth and my *"self-moment"* that I realized that we all see the world differently, and that I'm not always right.

Now this may sound crazy, but I believe that if I can own it, hopefully more of us will do the same. Once I accepted that I'm not always right and that I don't know everything, a strange thing happened to me. I began to feel really bad. I began to hurt at the notion that someone felt that their feelings were inferior to mine. Though it was never my intention to offend the person, I needed to first seek forgiveness from them. I had to reconstruct my years of doing things my way. I needed to take time to reassure the other person that their feelings are important to me, and that they're respected. Without taking the time to manage my role in relationships, I would still believe that my feelings were the only things that mattered. It is obvious that a relationship consists of 2 or more individuals. I can also say that maybe, just maybe that little portion of the guilt that I imposed on others because they didn't see things my way, may have been misguided as well. I had to apologize to myself because I never made room in my thinking to ever be wrong.

As easy as that may sound, it would take me a minute before I would truly learn the power and importance of forgiving myself. I had to take a *"self-moment"* and accept that we all make mistakes in life. It was in that mistake that I realized that I gave an emotional designation of guilt to a negative event. It was through that subconscious emotional assignment that I felt the need to nurture that pain and hold on to it. I had to come to the realization that I must free myself from that emotional entrapment if I am to regain control over my life. I had to be willing to accept the things that I couldn't change and realize that the offense doesn't define the totality of who I truly am; nor does it define my offender.

It must be noted that forgiveness requires a conscious willingness to forgive the offender. It's not up to that individual who offended me to seek my forgiveness. It is up to me to not allow their offense to dominate my emotions. A major part of forgiveness is that I must allow myself to live free of the offender and their offense. The longer it took for me to forgive that person, the worse off my health became. I got stressed very easily whenever I was in their presence or even by the mere mention of their name. Internally, I would get tense thinking that if I could only hide my feelings, they would never know the depth of my non-forgiveness. It wasn't until I went to my doctor that he began doing multiple tests on me trying to find out the cause of my high blood pressure, lack of sleep, and my overly reactive responses. After a very careful review and study of my behavior, nutrition, and inability to emotionally cope with tense situations; my doctor surmised that I was holding on to things that I should let go. Once I became honest with my feelings and the things that I was battling, the negative energy began to dissipate. My health improved.

Secondly, I learned that forgiveness must begin in the heart. There wasn't going to be a specific time, event, or warning sign that one would give to let me know that they are genuinely seeking my forgiveness. I must initiate within my own being that their actions will not alter my beliefs or permanently leave me in a state of discomfort. Once I accept the fact that I'm willing to forgive them, I then have to cosign on the path of forgiveness. Just as bereavement is a process, so is forgiveness.

I'm reminded of an incident that taught me a lot about the power and beauty within forgiveness. I was helping one of my mentees who was at a crossroad in her life. She came to me seeking advice on how she should approach her dilemmas. Her first challenge was that she had major issues with her mother. For many years she felt that her mother spent too much time trying to be her friend and not enough work at being her parent. As she reflected on her past, she said that her mother allowed her to get away with most things that she shouldn't have. Upon listening to her, I followed my first instinct. I redirected her back to her mother. Without a pause, she quickly told me how that wasn't an option. She further eluded that it's because of her mother that she's in the position that she's in.

I was forced to consider how to speak to a child without disrespecting their parent. Deep within me the words of forgiveness kept screeching through my mind. I knew that forgiveness would be only part of the journey that she had to travel in order to get some control of her life. The more she spoke, the more I kept hearing a wounded little girl who was trapped in the body of this blossoming young lady. I thought about Dr. John Bradshaw's Infancy Syndrome and how he explained that we're all just older children carrying the pain of our past. I know that with my limitations of not being a professional counselor, she would need assistance that I just could not offer.

I directed her to seek professional counseling. As soon as that was offered, I began to see tears form in the corners of her eyes. While knowing my limitations in helping her, I still asked, *"What's wrong?"* She began sobbing, talking about the entirety of her personal life. She ended the conversation letting me know that she needed a job. Without any reservation, I sought to put a bandage on the wound. Even though I knew that there was much more to this puzzle than what was before me, my heart began to weep at the thought of her pain. Therefore, I instructed her to mail me her resume. Upon receiving it, I made a couple of calls, and one of my contacts was willing to interview her for a lead position in their company. Problem solved, nope! That was only the beginning of the next cycle of events.

Excited and anxiously awaiting the news about her pending interview and job, I never received a call from her. The call that I received was from the pending manager who interviewed her. She alerted me that my mentee contacted her over that previous weekend, leaving a long crying voice message on her phone. At the very last minute, my mentee declined the job offer stating that she had too many family issues pending. Quietly and embarrassed I listened to the manager as she shared the message with me. I extended my apologies to her for any inconveniences that occurred and reminded her how much I valued her for the consideration.

While awaiting my mentee to call me, I began to have flashbacks to when I was an emotional wreck. Within my spirit,

I began to have nothing but sorrow for her. I knew that personally I couldn't help her with her emotional struggles. The first thing that I thought of was to offer her counseling. Though it would take nearly 2 weeks before I spoke with her regarding her last-minute job refusal, I was still determined to help her. Upon speaking, she didn't offer to go into her decision for refusing the job. What she offered to share with me was how the job wasn't a good fit for her. I asked her why she felt that way? She attempted to answer me with round about stories that had nothing to do with the question. Despite of the many rejections to counseling, I realized that prayer was the best thing that I could do.

All of my life I've heard the phrase *"you can lead a horse to water, but you can't make him drink."* It could not have been any simpler than that. She was not going to go to counseling until she felt ready to seek help. When I was battling my own demons, I didn't have someone offering me direction. It wasn't until I ended up in the hospital, embarrassed by the choices that I made for myself, that I was confronted with psychological help. I too stayed in denial. I hated everything and everyone with the same passion that I loved them. What I realized most was after I started the counseling process, is that I hated myself. It would take me some time before I would understand that a large part of my present emotions were birthed from my past childhood experiences. Knowing this to be certain, my mentee has a long road ahead of her.

My stumbling blocks for my healing had to do with my failure to identify the root of my ills. What became more apparent to me was that I kept rehearsing over and over the pains that I felt were wrongfully committed against me as a child. Once my psychotherapist was able to help me identify some of the roots to my dilemmas, I realized that hurting people, hurt people. I began to do as much study and research into the past of the person who offended me, than I was doing for myself. It wasn't too long that I would muster the nerve and energy to confront my offender. To my surprise, he was just as much a victim as I. He was the product of his environment and upbringing. He too was physically and psychologically abused, abandoned, and neglected. He carried years of baggage from his childhood. Just as psychologist John Bradshaw taught, *"We are all children, just older; carry the pains of our childhood."* In all honesty, because I loved him, I began to feel sorry for him. I was able to see his trapped child inside of his unhappy adult's body. All of my years of counseling had to kicked in. This is why I state that forgiveness isn't always easy. You have to want to offer it to someone. It was then that I chose to forgive him in order for me to move forward with my healing.

Finally, as I reflect on the issues with my mentee, I wanted to hold and reassure her that with help things would get better. After attending counseling for a few years, I had to reach back and rescue that child that lived inside of me. I had to go find him, then let him know that he is safe, valued, needed, and loved. I wrote him a letter ensuring him that the man that I am today can protect him. I only wanted that for her too. Once she's able to get to the root of her issues, she can then begin the process of healing and forgiving.

UNPACKING ONE ITEM AT A TIME

FORGIVENESS

The day will come when you recognize

That forgiveness is the only way back.

Iyanla Vanzant

UNPACKING ONE ITEM AT A TIME

CHAPTER 4

FEAR

While spending much of my time wondering why people wear masks, I cannot separate from the idea that the need for the mask represents an outward expression of fear. A mask tends to hide an image, face, or representation of something that one feels the need to conceal. They are most often associated with holidays, particularly worn for Halloween celebrations. Halloween is the acceptable time of the year in which millions of Americans are gifted the right to publicly conceal their images for the sake of entertainment. Historically, masks have been worn to pay homage to a civilization's ancestors, animals of the land, and God-like symbolisms. Masks are also used when individuals commit crimes. It can be seen on stores and bank cameras, where the establishment is being robbed by masked bandits. It is the hope of these bandits that their true identities are not revealed.

If we were to take a moment and think about the masked bandits, in spite of brandishing weapons, we can conclude that they possess fear. Their fear is built upon the notion of being exposed, recognized, hurt or caught, and sent to prison. We can also conclude that their use of masks has moral implications. They don't want their families, friends, and the public seeing them doing something morally wrong. While their actions may not be justified, their fear may be warranted.

I would like to delve further into the hidden fear that many of us face. Fear can be defined as a perceived danger or threat. It does not mean that something is about to happen that may cause another bodily harm. It is clearly based on the individual's perception, or how they feel about their present circumstances. There are 3 things that fear can cause an individual to do. It will either propel you to freeze, flight, or fight. That can be either good or bad considering the circumstance. We all face many types of fear that either propels us to do something productive and positive; or cause us to act inappropriately based on our emotions and reactions to fear. Fear can also paralyze our actions, causing many of us to fall short of our dreams. How often have you faced a dilemma where you chose not to act based on the fear of your vulnerabilities being exposed?

Whenever I think about what perceived danger constitutes as it applies to understanding fear, law enforcement immediately comes to mind. Across many of America's inner-city communities, there have been uprising protests that lead to violent encounters between law enforcement and the community. Over the past few years, there have been quite a few public cases where unarmed Americans of African descent have died at the hands of armed police officers.

Some of those cases involved the following individuals: Amadou Diallo, Manuel Loggins Jr., Ronald Madison, Kendra James, Sean Bell, Eric Garner, Michael Brown and Alton Sterling to name a few. Many of the armed law enforcement officers claimed that their choice to use lethal force was a direct consequence of their perceived fear. Whether or not we agree with their position of killing unarmed individuals, we must assert that a negative fear will likely propel one to commit atrocious and at times lethal actions against others.

I've been closely following recent reports of crimes against humanity that have been occurring in Libya for many years. Often, I wonder what could possibly cause the majority of any people to resign their power and rights to the minority. I'm always lead back to fear. Fear has been the tactic of Arabs who enforced slavery by using fear to sell, abuse, and at times kill the African detainees in Libya. The detainees' fear is birthed from shock, torture, displacement, lack of opportunities, and the unknown. Since the 2011 American lead overthrow of Libya's leader Muammar Gaddafi's government, rebel soldiers have enslaved African migrants all for the sake of individual economic gain. Enslaving and selling African migrants on trading blocs have become one of the country's foremost leading economic booms.

After watching these atrocities on television, social media, and reading about them in print; I found myself questioning my ability to conquer my own fears. One may ask, what fears might I have as it pertains to the plight of the African migrants in Libya? My response is simple, *I am my brother's keeper*. In addition to that, life has taught me that history has a way of repeating itself. The bearers of moral justice must be willing to put their fears aside, and fight for everyone's civil justice and human rights. Should I allow my fears of what others may think of me, lost wages, being arrested, fined, or even hurt paralyze me from acting on behalf of my African brothers and sisters who are enslaved in Libya? If so, my voice would never articulate their plight.

On the afternoon of Wednesday, November 29, 2017, I was lead to the Libyan Embassy in New York, to join the protests against Libyan traffickers who were detaining African migrants. Upon my arrival I was surprised to see the barricades folded off to the side and that there was no one protesting. To say that I was surprised by this lack of protest would be an understatement. Immediately I became very paranoid and afraid. It was my intention to join in a movement that had passion, purpose, and the protection of national media. The media's presence at this protest would have guaranteed that my actions of civil disobedience be captured on some form of media, which would ensure my overall safety. Not having my personal safety guaranteed, was reason for alarm.

As I pulled up in front of the building next to the Libya House Embassy, I first noticed that the car in front of me had a bright yellow boot lock on its tire. I could only wonder if I was at the correct address. Without hesitation I googled the Embassy, only to realize that I was at the correct location. One thing about fear that I eluded to earlier, was that it has the ability to freeze you in your tracks, forcing you to ignore what's in front of you. In this case, I immediately had to calculate a plan that would surmount my fears. Then I thought about writer Joyce Meyer who suggested to *"Do it afraid."* I began taking pictures of the front of the Embassy with hopes of writing this juicy post against the Libyan Government.

While standing on the landing of the Embassy building, I saw a hurried security guard heading my way. The quicker he approached, the quicker my plan went into action. I began filming myself with my cellphone camera with hopes of recording any actions that I may encounter. As he exited the building to confront me, asking *"How can I help you?"* I entered through the other glass door with my camera rolling to ensure my safety while in the building. He re-entered the building asking me the same question. I knew that though I was afraid, I still had a mission to accomplish. I chose not to answer his questions, but instead raise my own, *"Is this the Libyan Embassy? Is this the Office of His Excellency Ambassador Elmahdi S. Elmajerbi?"* Once I got confirmation that I was at the correct location, I immediately told the guard that I had a meeting with him.

While he looked for my name in the database; and as the Embassy workers were entering and exiting the building, I raised my tone of questioning. I asked why were the barricades folded outside the building's entrance and pushed off to the side? He responded, *"That was some protest from yesterday."* Immediately thereafter, he looked at me, informing me that my name was not on the roster for a meeting. He also stated that the Ambassador does not take unscheduled visits from walk-ins. I demanded that he provide me with a number so that I could call and schedule a meeting with the Ambassador of which he obliged. As he was writing the number for the offices of the Embassy, my fears propelled me to leave a lasting impression on him and everyone present. I began shouting *"How is it that in 2017 your Libyan government condones the violation of the human rights of African migrants in Libya? How is it that your government condones slavery, human trafficking and the selling of human beings for the sake of individual economic wealth?"* As I continued in my rant, *doing it afraid*, the security officer and another gentleman walked from behind their desk to escort me out of the Embassy. Upon leaving the facility, I realized that in order for any form of justice to prevail, I knew that I had to overcome my fears.

Author Joyce Meyer's *Fear Principle* of *"Do It Afraid,"* has become my approach whenever I'm confronted by fear. Through her approach, I cannot give into unhealthy fears. She suggests that we need to have courage in the face of fear and adversity. By her definition, courage is defined as *"progress in the face of fear."* Therefore, *"confrontation is necessary for freedom."* Her references to God through many scriptures in the Bible, tends to suggest that one should make a declaration stating that *"I will not fear."*

Interestingly enough and prior to my reading of her philosophy on fear, I too practiced a similar approach. When I'm leaving my office building from a long day at work, it is usually somewhere around 2 a.m. My office is not in the safest neighborhood that one could choose. In actuality, it is situated in a high crime district of an urban city. The security cameras that I have placed around my building are often used by the local police for solving crimes that are committed just feet from my door. Should I live in fear, I would never leave my office. I clearly remember one evening, somewhere around 3:00 a.m. when I decided to leave the building. Conscious of the possibility of potential crimes and danger in the neighborhood, I tend to leave cautiously. This one summer evening as I was locking up the building, I looked around as I normally do for suspicious traffic and activities. Once I saw that the area was clear and free of danger, I began to walk to my car. Unbeknownst to me, a huge man appeared at my rear and brushed up against me with no regard. Though I didn't outwardly show it, I was frightened beyond measure.

At that point and every day that followed, I had to dig deep within myself. I had to choose whether or not I would live in fear. Many would state that fear is false evidence appearing real. Was it the man's intent to do bodily harm to me, even though he forcefully brushed up against me? Or, was I so nervous and caught off guard that the fear I had was *incidental fear*. Incidental fear limits itself to the present threat that may cause anxieties. Once the threat is gone, so is the fear. Perceiving my situation as just incidental, I continued to leave the building guarded, but not afraid. What I choose to do is speak life over my emotions that may perpetuate the feelings of fear. Nightly from the time I cut off the lights and lock my doors, I recite Psalm 23 which states *"The Lord is my shepherd, I shall not want......I fear no evil...:"* It is through this affirmation, similar to that of Meyer's declaration of *"I will not fear"* that I boldly leave my office, *"doing it afraid."* By pushing through my fears, I'm conquering and bringing under subjection my emotions. The more often that I practice this principle, my confidence increases.

Simultaneously, I'm reminded of my years and experiences of being an entrepreneur. As an entrepreneur, I'm faced with many uncertainties every day. It's my sole responsibility to earn a living for myself and those who I employ. In spite of fear, I must face all of the uncertainties that come with the responsibility of ownership. If I don't take the risk of being creative and forever looking at opportunities for success, I, nor my businesses would have flourished. Many folks fail in their pursuit of business success because they're afraid to take risks. The whole idea of risk-taking requires one to have a certain level of self-assurance that their inclinations are greater than the odds pitted against them. This leads me to think of how many folks are afraid of success.

One of the key components of success is change. People by and large, fear change. Change is not soothing because often it brings feelings of anxiety and uncertainty. Change requires action! Just as Meyer alluded through the affirmation of *"I will not fear,"* change forces one to take actions that counter their emotions of fear. If I viewed fear through the history of my experiences, I would not have succeeded in business to the degree in which I have. Prior to me entering into the world of business, I hadn't seen nor met too many entrepreneurs. I remember asking my Dad about his feelings of entrepreneurship, he couldn't relate to it. He was from a generation of African Americans becoming first time homeowners in northern cities. His generation went to a job, punched in at a clock, and worked for 8.5 hours, 5 days a week. The idea of believing that you can create your own opportunities were not in his mind. He began to question why I wouldn't want to get a job with benefits and raises, and why would I want to tackle those unnecessary responsibilities of owning a business? He spoke in depth with me about his perceived challenges. In all of what he had to say, I summed up his fear, lack of willingness to confront it; and his lack of self confidence in conquering a personal goal.

I was further challenged by a senior male who had a second-hand hosiery business. I asked him about the pros and cons of being an entrepreneur. To my surprise, he shut me down. He described his business as a hustle and discouraged me from thinking independently about my sources of income. As I began to question him more about his rationale for not speaking to the pros of entrepreneurship, he said it's like smoking mirrors. It was he who first told me about the percentages of small businesses that succeed in today's marketplace. It was he who made me do research and study why businesses fail. After compiling 2 months of research and data, I went back to him with questions. Even though I had a thought as to why he didn't want to talk to me about entrepreneurship, I continued to push. From our conversation, he became humbled. After taking many pauses and breaths while speaking, he told me that he didn't want me to end up like him. The way I saw him was far different from the way he saw himself.

I have always seen this man as a successful, content individual who was at peace with what he was doing. Though he had a fulltime job, I saw his side business as something that he had always dreamed of doing fulltime. After speaking with him, he informed me that he felt like he failed himself in his career. When asked why he felt that way, he said that he feared failing his family. He didn't think that his second hand business would support the financial needs of his family. He was like so many individuals who gave up on their dreams for fear of failure. I could only wonder if he were to make a sincere, concerted effort at developing his business plan, he might have known if it would have worked.

Far too often, many folks give up on their dreams because of fear. How often have you heard someone speak about the *"would have, could have"* stories? Many work and spend a lifetime in jobs that they are not satisfied with. They beat themselves up unnecessarily with regrets of not moving on an idea, feeling or thought that they had. They've allowed their emotions to dominate and kill the pursuit of their dreams. Experience has taught me that the acceptance of failure is the first step to success. If you don't make an attempt to change your present condition, then you'll be left in the same location of complaints, dissatisfaction, and frustration. Many have watched me open up company after company, but little did they know about the many failures that I faced. Through a very small incident I learned that if I should fail/fall in my attempt at a goal, that I could get back up and try it again.

It was the first time that I went skiing. I went there with 3 of my friends, all of whom stated that they had previous experience on the slopes. I was the only one who never put on skis a day in my life. Before I go any further, let me not fail to mention that I was the only African American in this group of skiers. You may wonder how that plays into this equation.

Growing up poor in the inner city, we were not exposed to many extracurricular activities. We didn't have the luxury of playing in organized water sports, nor any type of winter activities. Our only two water sports came in the height of the summer when our neighbor's father would take his big monkey wrench and open the fire hydrant as we ran in front of the water to cool off. The other water sport was when my dad would allow the neighborhood kids to put on their swimming trunks and run in front of a water hose that he was holding. Those were the only water sports that we had. Many of the other sports that were played in the more affluent communities, we were not exposed to. We as young inner city kids had to become creative with our sports. Therefore, we thrived at most athletic activities. Also, as the only African American in the group, I felt some kind of way with them pointing and telling me that I needed to get lessons. That hit me in the wrong place though I'm sure they meant nothing by it. For me, I became more determined to ski without any lessons. I told them to lead the way.

As I followed closely behind them, I realized they were not the best skiers that I thought they were. They began to fall before we even got to the bunny hop slopes. As I watched, I fought very hard at maintaining my balance. I was stiff as a board. It wasn't until I fell that I realized that it was only a short distance from the height of my stance to the ground I was walking on. In addition, each time that I fell, my confidence began to build even more. My fears of falling began to dissipate. I began to ski right through my fears of falling. It was the lesson of failure/falling that became the first part of my success of becoming a good skier. Had I not fallen, I never would have realized that I could get up, and I would have never tried skiing from the start. By the end of that evening, they were watching me with envy from their fallen positions as I skied past them down the steepest slopes and onto the next challenge.

Through the skiing example, it shows how to attain success through your fears. It carries a huge message. I'm reminded of a phrase that comedian Steve Harvey tells his audiences. He says, "In order to be successful, you have to jump." Even though he will be credited for that phrase, I have lived it. As previously stated, I closed down a few of my companies nearly 2 years ago. The emotional toll of processing the closing of those businesses weighed heavy on my heart. I found myself in a dilemma. If I keep them open, I'll continue to chase after the dollar and all of the stress that's required for maintaining that pace. If I close them, I am certain to face my fears of the unknown alone.

I remember one day while I was in the thick of my emotional struggles, I wanted to give up on everything. I no longer cared about my annual earnings of producing millions of dollars. I no longer cared about the many mouths that I was feeding by employing individuals from the community. I no longer cared about having the latest European automobiles or my collection of expensive antique cars. I no longer cared. Monthly, I faced making insurance premiums in excess of $30,000.00. Weekly, I was burdened with frivolous law suits, all for the sake of other's greed. Daily, I became emotionally exhausted fighting for the very individuals that I employed, even though I didn't feel appreciated.

One day I decided to follow the lead of one of my nieces. She and a couple of her college friends decided to go skydiving. I asked her about her reasoning for doing it. Her response was that she only did it because that was what her friends wanted to do. I saw skydiving as an opportunity for me to surmount my fears of the uncertainties that I was sure to face. I always had a fear of heights that exceeded two story buildings. Neither did I possess a fear of death, even though it's the biggest unknown. My fears were basic. They were mainly rooted in the possibility of me having to live with the consequences of my choice to close my companies. How would I survive? Would I be able to provide for my mom?

Those were my only concerns. After a 10-minute flight, my questions were answered.

It was a small Cessna plane that struggled to climb to nearly 15,000 feet. I sat cramped amongst strangers, with tears in my eyes. My emotions were trying to get the best of me. I was overwhelmed with the possibility that I was going to win the fight over my fears of uncertainty. I finally was going to face them. I began to think about how I drove 3 hours from my home just to be as far away from there as possible. I thought about my Mom and the toll it would have on her should she be left without me as a result of my actions. I thought about how I would no longer have to deal with the emotional toll of working around so much negative energy from some of the people that I worked with. I teared because every bit of me was willing to face an uncertain future without them. I didn't go there solely to return to the same nonsense. I went there to meet with God.

If skydiving can be used as a metaphor for the problems that I faced in life, then the actual leap can be best described as me casting all of my cares upon God. I used the idea of skydiving as a way to cast my fears, doubts, anger, frustrations, and concerns away, and trust that God will take care of me from this day forward. If taking the flight wasn't enough, I even wrote on my hands "Good Bye" for those who loved me would understand that I intentionally chose this approach.

Some of you who are reading this may question my approach to seeking an answer from God, as extreme. Please know that we all have our own crosses to bear. What you may need to get to where you're going, may not be what I needed to get to my destination; and besides, it may not get me anywhere. I affirm Steve's affirmation, "You have to jump." You have to jump from convenience and comfort, to the beauty of change, from being plagued with procrastination, to your journey of optimism; and from your past, to your future. In all, the measure of your faith will be the tool that you need to conquer your fears.

FEAR AND FAITH

Fear and faith have something in common.

They both ask us to believe in something we cannot see.

Joel Osteen

UNPACKING ONE ITEM AT A TIME

CHAPTER 5

INNER VOICE

By nature, we do not trust our inner voice. We write it off as just having an inclination of something. It is because there's no present valid evidence to support the claim, or the external influences tend to dissuade the thought. That non-trusting factor tends to leave us feeling frustrated and disappointed, especially when our inclinations turn out to yield favorable results. How often have you lived with the regrets of your decisions for not heeding the advice of that inner voice?

Unfortunately, most of us do not follow the urges of our inclinations because of pre-existing circumstances. Before I sought counseling for my many years of battling depression and low self-esteem issues, I was always living with regrets. I looked upon those thoughts as just passing feelings with no merit. When I compound the negative lenses through which I viewed myself and the pressure to choose a direction for my life, I could never trust my gut. At times I wondered if I was good enough, or whether or not what I had to say really mattered. In any case, my self-doubt was so great that it prevented me from acting on an urge to do so. The longer I stayed in my regretful state, the angrier I would become. I began to hate myself for not having enough confidence to know my value, and that I was worthy of loving myself a lot more. Though it would take years of therapy, eventually I was able to trust the voice in me.

To the contrary, I began to love the person I was after attending therapy. I started acting upon and trusting my inner voice. I began to listen to *it* as it became my subconscious reminder to past events and feelings. I remember receiving a call from a longtime friend of mine who was a Social Worker. She was trying to place mentally ill consumers within the workplace of local businesses. Prior to her asking me to hire certain individuals with pre-existing mental conditions, I probably would have never considered it. I'm sure that at the time I was like most people; we think of the stereotypical image of what mentally ill people would look or even act like. It took a minute for me to contemplate every bad thing that could go wrong before I would be awakened by my thoughts to go against my fears. Trusting that my inner voice would not fail me, I chose to hire not only 1 but 3 individuals with pre-existing mental health conditions. It was my belief that forced me to move behind my fears. I put focus on what would happen to them should I not hire them. To date, that willingness to trust and listen to my inner voice has been one of the most fulfilling rewards. I can say I've benefited the most by making that decision.

While I can list many instances where I trusted my inner voice, I won't bore you. I find it very interesting whenever I speak to someone who acts upon their intuition, even when they can't understand why they felt a certain way towards that person. Just yesterday I was speaking with a very good friend of mine about some actions he had taken against his sister's new boyfriend. He and his sister share a 3-bedroom apartment. After working a full 8-hour workday, he would come home to fix himself something to eat, then try and relax. Daily his sister would have this same guy visiting her, who she never claimed as anything more than just a friend. Not that it matters the intimacy status of her relationship, the brother was troubled by the presence of her guest being there every day. Time after time he would come home and completely ignore his sister's company. One day his sister asked him why he treats her guest a certain way? He could only respond, *"There's something about him that I just don't like."* When I pushed him to elaborate a little further he said, *"I just can't put my finger on it."*

It's this phrase that gets so many of us in trouble. *"There's something about him that I just don't like...I just can't put my finger on it."* As crazy as this may sound, so many of us experience this very thing. It's that instinct that drives us to settle on decisions that are based on emotions that are not grounded upon any one definitive fact. Quite often, we allow these inclinations to determine our actions and outcomes, even if they seem to make us appear as though we're losing our minds.

For the sake of continuing this story, I'll refer to the offender as "brother," while the offended remains "sister."

The brother began telling me his version of what happened in his household last Thursday evening after working overtime on his job. He said that *by the time he got home, he was tired and hungry and just wanted to rest. He was exhausted by the day's events.* He's a Correctional Officer at the local state prison. He guards prisoners who are in some cases serving life sentences for murder. He began to share with me how one of the inmates began to hallucinate, causing violent outbursts against other prisoners and the guards had to restrain him. He was forced to become physical with this huge, muscular inmate. Even after being restrained, they still had to exert physical and mental energy in order to get him tied to the stretcher for transport to the local hospital. After such a full day of events, coming home to company was not something that he was hoping to see.

As a brief note about his sister, she's a couple of years his senior and has been out of work due to a terrible accident that she had while on her job. She was an EMT, transporter of critically ill patients. One early morning while she and her coworker were transporting one of their patients, her coworker fell asleep at the wheel. This forced the ambulance to hit several parked cars. Although the driver and patient were securely strapped down in a stretcher and were not injured, the same could not be said about his sister. His sister had taken off her seating restraints to perform a blood pressure check on the patient. No sooner than the ambulance hit the parked cars, she was thrown to the front of the driver's compartment of the vehicle. Even though the accident occurred 2 years prior, it left her permanently disabled and with a short-ended career as an EMT. She was forced to have back surgery, where she ended up with a 16-inch rod positioned along her spine that would later paralyze much of her lateral movements. It also left her personal life in shambles. Her then husband abandoned her for a younger suitor, claiming that she could no longer perform her wifely duties. Not too concerned from where the attention came, she sought companionship.

With all of that said, this story is about how someone who did not have concrete evidence was able to listen, trust, and then act upon the inclinations of his inner voice. Often most of us do not trust our gut, in this instance the brother did. He said that he was determined to address his sister's friend if he was in the house upon his arrival home. The sister and her friend were in the kitchen playing a board game. Without any prodding, the brother entered the kitchen and tossed aside the board game that the sister and her company were playing. He began to tell me as though he was getting a rise by bragging to me how he sent all of the game pieces flying in the air and then to the floor. Alarmed by her brother's actions, the sister immediately confronted the brother. Not wanting to get involved in a fight with the brother, the friend chose to exit the kitchen and head towards the front door. There he was confronted by the brother. The two of them began fighting and tussling until the friend pulled out a knife and began to repeatedly superficially stab the brother who was on top of him. While watching the fight, the sister got involved by wrestling the knife out of her friend's hand.

This story could have ended horribly. While I do not condone the actions of the brother, a lot must be said when we can heed to the inner voice that triggers urges of familiarity to an event or place. Two weeks later the validity of listening to his inner voice would pay off. One day while working at the prison, a coworker called the brother over. He informed him that an inmate requested not to be in the same cell area that he patrolled. Believing that he was an even tempered and well-liked individual by his coworkers and clients, the brother couldn't figure out why someone wouldn't want to work with him. Upon looking at the cameras to see who the person was who launched the complaint against him, he noticed a familiar face. Sitting in the cell with his head down was his sister's friend, a new inmate to the jail. The brother decided to break all work protocol and enter the area where the inmate was sitting just to tell him, *"You don't have to hide your face from me. I already know who you are."*

The brother eagerly exited the area where the inmate was being detained. For the rest of that workday and with excitement in his stride, the brother couldn't wait to get home to inform his sister that her friend was an inmate at his facility. Bursting through the door of his workplace at the end of his day, the brother had only one thing on his mind. As he was telling me this story, his excitement began to bubble up again as though he was reliving the events of that day. On his way home, he said that he began to rehearse his sister's responses in his head. He began with, *"If she says this, Imma say that."* He ran into his home saying, *"I told you that I knew that joker from somewhere else. I told you!"* Surprised by his approach, the sister said, *"Who are you talking about?"* "Your *boyfriend is a prisoner at my facility."* He went on to tell her the details of his day, even though she didn't seem concerned or surprised. By the time he finished telling her, she just strolled away as though nothing happen.

After telling me this story, I could only wonder if he felt bad about his actions without having any tangible proof prior to support his feelings. Quickly he responded to me saying, *"Though it appears that my actions were not right, I have no regret because I listened to my inner voice. It's never wrong!"* I paused in my response to him. I stood there waiting for him to tell me something else or maybe come up with another explanation to justify his actions. To my surprise, he stood firm and committed to his actions and belief. If I were to surmise the actions of the brother I would not hesitate to say that though he couldn't substantiate his opinions of his sister's friend, deep inside he knew that there was something wrong with that guy.

Though he couldn't put an exact face, name, or bring clarity to their past experience, he did not discount the power of the subconscious. Somewhere in his subconscious, there was a subliminal note made of the man's posture, facial features and/or movements. This subconscious marker was recalled upon the first day that the brother saw the gentleman in his kitchen with his sister. What is interesting about the recalling factor of the subconscious mind is that I'm reminded of the autocorrect settings on my computer. Most times it is accurate with correcting the spelling, grammar, or word choice. There are times that it replaces the misspelled word with similarly spelled words that have some relevance to the sentence but is the wrong tense. Though this occurs, the accuracy of its recalling ability is phenomenal.

Have you ever met someone and couldn't recall where you met them? Have you ever heard the story of that friend who is now bearing witness to how they didn't listen to their inner voice regarding dating someone who turned out to be no good for them? What about the case where your inner voice told you not to drive down a road; and you end up in an accident because you didn't listen to that voice that told you otherwise.

Unfortunately, it's that same inner voice that often leads to much confusion, mistrust, doubting, and even fighting in relationships. The girlfriend has thoughts that the boyfriend has engaged in infidelities. She has no concrete evidence to support her claim. She just feels it within. We've all heard the phrases, *"Something ain't right or I just can put my finger on it, but..."* Upon her confronting him with her suspicions about his infidelity, he breaks the cardinal rule by putting the infidelity allegations on her. Because of her suspicions and lack of trust for her boyfriend, the couple ends up fighting and breaking off their relationship. In the case of the couple who begins to fight and eventually break things off, it was for the good of both. Who wants to be in a relationship where your mate does not trust you? In addition, who wants to be in a relationship where you're accused of doing something that you have no knowledge of? Whether it's worked to your advantage or not, is not the issue. A person who is well trained at listening to their inner voice is more likely to be accurate on their intuition than inaccurate. The question that I raise is whether or not that voice is solely based on a feeling or subconscious reminder of a conscious experience.

If we venture back to the story of the brother and sister, I believe that the feelings of discomfort that he experienced upon seeing his sister's friend in the house was largely due to a subconscious reminder of a conscious experience. The conscious experience that the brother had was brought to the forefront of his mind because of a previous interaction that they shared. Their first visual connection came in a hostile environment, the brother's workplace. The brother views the prison and those incarcerated through a negative lens. Therefore, when his subconscious reminder alerted him to a familiar face that he could not place at the time, the negative connotation appeared. This doesn't mean that the brother knew the boyfriend. What it shows is that the subconscious has it photographic catalog of faces, experiences and locations.

Throughout my adult life, I have made substantial business investments of which some were huge losses, while others paid consistent dividends. In the cases where I chose not to listen to my inner voice, those were my biggest business losses to date. I noticed that when my heart, ego, and everything that controls my emotional side became a large part of my decision-making process, those were often my worst financial times in business. One of the things that I learned is that our inner voices have power and we should take the time to study and learn how to listen to them. Sometimes acting upon our urges have no positive guarantees. Many folks still do, even though it isn't the most accurate method of gauging your successes or failures. It also offers the opportunity to pause from making rushed decision. Whenever you make a rushed decision while engaging in a real-time situation, you are more likely to end up with unfavorable results.

As I consider my techniques for listening to my inner voice, I cannot separate God from the thought process. In every faith, one has the choice to listen to one's subconscious voice. God gifted me with the blessing of vision. With it, I'm able to create and develop enterprises that have provided jobs for many in the community. At one point in my business portfolio, I had 7 companies running at the same time that employed nearly 60 people. All of these companies were birthed from little ideas that I had running around in my head. Had I not trusted the intuition of my inner voice, I would not have been able to put a dent in the unemployment market that plagues the inner city communities from where I come.

Alex Lickerman MD, author of the book *"The Undefeatable Mind: On the Science of Constructing an Indestructible Self (HCI),"* recently weighed in on his opinion of how to make intuitive decisions. He first suggests that we become better at trusting our instincts. We must not yield to the distrusting factors of our internal complex machinery that brought us to the thought and/or inclination. We tend not to trust it because of the rapid rate by which these inclinations flow and function. He suggests that we are experts at reading each other's behaviors. We need to pay more attention to controlling the influences of our biases, fears, and our own pathology regarding the intentions of others.

To become better at making intuitive decisions, he suggests that you *"Pause"* before making rushed decisions. He alludes that most decisions do not warrant immediate responses. Therefore, he suggests that you use phrases as *"I need to think about this."* This would afford you the needed time to think about what's going on, and why you may be experiencing uncomfortable feelings. Secondly, he says to *"listen"* to your body. Often when uncomfortable with a decision, your body may experience levels of discomfort. It is in this time of discomfort that you should make mental notes to compare past similar discomforting signs when making similar present decisions. Finally, he suggests that you *"Hone Your Instincts."* Get in the habit of heeding to the process of past successful results when you've listened to your inner voice.

There were times when I didn't trust my inner voice during the startup of my many companies. I allowed my insecurities to get in the way of trusting a decision that I needed to make. I first wrestled with the thought of what if I failed in my attempt and lost everything that I invested? I've always believed that our emotions of doubt are birthed from true places of experiences. At times, we may have failed at things and never once took the time to examine why. Unfortunately, we tend to establish our fears based on that one failed experience rather than the success of the process. This in turn opens our doors of self-doubt and insecurities. If someone asked why you failed in your attempt, it is so easy to blame it on everything and everyone except for ourselves. Deep within, one may argue that in this instance that the person should have listened to their inner voice which told them to pursue the goal. If someone blames their failures on listening to their inner voice, they should also raise the questions as to what plan of action did they establish to meet the anticipated goal?

Years ago, I sold Amway products. Back then a team of my colleagues would meet in a local hotel's main conference room. There, we would invite guests who we thought shared our vision for a more secured financial future. Though I never reached the highest pinnacle of those gem designations that were based on my network of sales, I still was afforded the opportunity to eat off of the revenue that I generated. In front of a packed audience of curious guests, there was a monitor that introduced the "head honcho" of that branch. Afterwards they would play a follow-up video that showed financial promises with soothing music and nicely edited footage. I bring Amway into this conversation because once I joined the company through my local network, many of the presenters opened their presentations with the catch phrase, *"People don't plan to fail. They fail to plan."* As simple as this phrase is, it is by far the most honest statement that explains failure that one would encounter than any other statement that I've heard to date.

While planning and succeeding have an illicit relationship, it is important to note that the failure rate of most businesses is greater than the success rate. In the execution of any idea, plan, or even test, we must develop a plan of action. It is standard procedure to have a "Business Plan" upon creating any business. In order for your business plan to be successful, you must trust your instincts while eliminating your emotions. Similar to Dr. Lickerman suggestion, emotions and fears are likely contradictions to the success of positive results when trusting your intuition. Business plans are used as structured roadmaps that lay down the vision, competition, needs and demographics of a specific territory. A good business plan is necessary when one seeks a business loan to grow their particular business. A lender wants to see the actual data, finances, vision, and experience of the individual/organization who seeks to borrow money. Should one not be able to produce a plan of action or "Business Plan," they reduce the likelihood of the lender to loan them money.

The importance and value of having a plan is immeasurable. Whether or not you move forward with the execution of that plan is only secondary to having one. Having a plan affords you a greater likelihood of succeeding in the business you're seeking to open or expand. Statistics show in many of our business periodicals a high percentage of companies that close their doors by the end of its 3rd business year. There are even more staggering numbers for the amount of businesses that last beyond the 3rd year. Most of these businesses that failed on the basis of the Amway quote of *"People don't plan to fail. They fail to plan."* When we put the responsibility of our failures on everything except for the failure to plan, we will never understand why we fail.

When we add the idea of listening to your inner voice when making decisions, that voice can be heard as a subconscious reminder of an actual experience, even if it fails. Failure for me has been nothing short of experience that I've learned to archive in the back of my mind. Have you ever been reminded of an experience that allowed your brain to catalogue an event that may have happened a long time ago? That event may have made a positive or negative impression on you. In any case, you were able to reference the experience when faced with a similar situation. That has happened to me throughout my business career. So, when I'm at a point of determining whether or not I should invest in a business concept, it is with that same inner voice that steers my decision.

Until a person shows me rude or negative behavior, I accept them freely without judgement. If I allowed my inner voice to be silenced and never trusted my instincts based solely on me having tangible evidence to support my belief, then I would not have been as successful in business. As an entrepreneur, I had to rely on others to get the job done. It wasn't me driving the bus, picking up the patients, or dropping off the students to and from school. I had to entrust supervisors who made my life easier. They were the ones on the front line ensuring the daily running of the companies, not me. I created and managed the leadership of the companies and not the workers. I allowed their methodology to prevail with the daily decision making of the employees as long as no one's rights were violated or laws broken.

There were times when I've hired individuals with checkered pasts. The person was first interviewed by my manager who refused to hire them. The manager then brought me the application for review stating their concerns. In that application I saw a few questionable answers that would discourage the average person from employing them. I asked the manager to review the application with me and tell me the foundation of their concerns. They pointed out the fact that the person listed a PO Box and also checked "yes" in the box for the question, *"Have you ever been arrested?"* The manager's explanation was that they didn't want to have a criminal working in close quarters in this office. I paused and thought about it for a minute. Before I could discard the application in the pile of *"would have been employees,"* I asked the manager if she questioned the applicant regarding their answer. The manager immediately said, *"What for? They already told you what they about. Besides, he listed a PO Box instead of an actual mailing address for his residence."* This alone was not a good enough reason for me not to consider hiring this person. Half of the employees of my companies stole money, time, supplies, and resources on a daily basis.

When looking further into the application, I noticed that the person kept their previous job for over 15 years, and only left because the company went out of business. That was a positive sign of a reliable and dedicated employee. Not only were they a reliable candidate, they had outstanding leadership skills of which were lacking with my present company. It wasn't until the applicant was interviewed by me and the manager, did the applicant offer an explanation for their arrest. The arrest was due to nonpayment of child support. To explain the gap in employment, he went on to say that after the unemployment ran out, he ended up in a homeless shelter, which explained why he didn't have an actual address. After the interview I asked my manger if they changed their opinion on hiring the individual, their response was simply *"No!"* If I were to just look at the person based on what is before me, I probably would never had considered them for hire either.

It was the power and trust of my inner voice that spoke the loudest to me. It was as though I was making a choice that differed from what my rational mind told me to do. Everything about his application was grounds for me to move on to the next candidate. It was solely because I listened to that inner voice, that for the next 7 years, that homeless employee became my personal assistant and has lead the way to our company securing many large contracts. Most folks doubt the power of their inner voice. Trust me; I am totally in agreement with that because I didn't always listen to mine. Just as with most things, one has to learn how to hone in on the accuracy of their inner voice. It has come with practice that I've become more comfortable with trusting mine.

When one studies a guide book for answering multiple choice questions, there's a process of elimination that narrows your scope to make a more accurate decision. The first step is to eliminate those things that have nothing to do with the question. Once eliminated, it should no longer weigh in your decision-making process.

The next thing that I learned is not to make emotional decisions. I use to allow my emotions to dictate my actions. If I felt a certain way about things and my subconscious wanted to move in a different direction, I'd use that as a time to meditate, then think things through. By doing that, I could usually pinpoint what makes me question its validity. I should be able to understand why I had that negative vibe when I first looked at the situation. That would then allow me to make a more informed decision. This is also seen in my substance abuse clinic where our motto is *"Meet people where they are."* Often when we are confronted with the emotions of an individual and not the issue, we tend to deal with the emotion. If we seek to understand the emotional side of things, we can then move to solving and treating the issue.

Finally, I ensure that I don't characterize every feeling that I have on common experiences. As a child, I developed a dislike and fear for eating fish. My dislike for eating fish was not due to the taste of it. It was based on me as a kid getting the bones stuck in my throat. When offered fish, I'd get a sour taste in my mouth causing my eyebrows to rise. I would even feel in the back of my throat the desire to regurgitate whenever I saw someone near me eating it. When offered, I'd immediately decline stating that I don't like fish. It took nearly 30 years before I would eat fish and enjoy the taste. For many years I allowed a childhood experience to overshadow an adult decision about something that I never realized I enjoyed. Even though I got sick by just the thought of having fish near me, I would later determine what was actually making me sick? Once I was able to understand that it wasn't the physical fish nor its smell that I hated, it was solely psychological with me. I allowed my fears of bones getting caught in my throat to manifest itself into an all-out phobia. Once you're willing to do the hard work and learn how to manage your emotions, especially when it comes to making choices for your life, it is then that you begin to rely on your inner voice.

I wasn't always willing to do the hard work. All of the external matters of life began to occupy my internal space. Our home was set on fire. We were homeless and lived in a welfare motel. My father was abusive whenever he was drunk. I was carjacked on my way to school. As you can see, I've had more than enough things on my plate that would consume my mind. Things that most folks didn't concern themselves with, I, on the other hand found my mind flooded with the emotional weight of my very being. I was heavily weighted down with issues of self-doubt that were plagued by long bouts with depression and self-imposed abuse. For many years, I just couldn't see my way through. Based on my inability to process my raw emotions, my glass was always half empty, as well as the skies were always cloudy. My low self-esteem kept me from trusting my inner voice. As that voice would be inclined to go in one direction, often I would make the opposite choice to go the other way. Most of my distrust was based on my low self-esteem and fears of failing, not only me but also others. I was more concerned with what others thought about my failures than me looking at them as opportunities to grow from. Finally, after years of learning how to trust my inner voice, the world that I saw appeared positive. It was that "inner voice" within that always sought to lead me in the right direction. It was the strength of overpowering *"Self-doubting voices"* that I needed to master in order to WIN.

UNPACKING ONE ITEM AT A TIME

My spirit tells me I cannot be silent.

Rep. Maxine Waters

UNPACKING ONE ITEM AT A TIME

CHAPTER 6

MASKING

I open up most of my presentations asking *"Is there a Hero in this room?"* Far too often, those that are present tend to either not respond, or just give me the kind smile and courteous nod. Knowing this to be their expected response, I use their uncertainties as leverage for my own apprehensions and fears. No matter how often I do this type of stuff, I still have residuals from my childhood insecurities in my bag of goodies. They keep my comfort level at a distance. In the back of my mind I'm wrestling with thoughts and hopes that I don't forget the basis of my presentation. Inwardly I'm stressing myself to the point where I begin to perspire. I use to wonder if anyone cared about what I had to say, or whether or not it had any value to them? Though these thoughts continue to enter my mind; I've learned how not to allow them to dominate the conversation that I'm having with myself. In doing so, I learned a technique for masking my feelings.

I've never considered the concept of masking because never did I feel the conscious need to do so. It wasn't until I began to share my personal thoughts, experiences, and expertise publicly that I noticed I had a reservoir of public speaking fears and apprehensions. In fact, I never saw myself to be much of a public speaker. Public speaking did not come naturally to me. I had to learn and develop coping strategies for successfully presenting before crowds of people. It took me a while before I accepted the fact that people have so much more in common than not. They are just as curious to learn about what I have to say, as I am equally eager to hear from them. The only difference between them and me is that I am the one holding the microphone. I listened to different *experts* as they instructed folks on how to be better public speakers. Each time I tried one of their techniques my nerves would still get the best of me. I tried over and over to convince myself that there was no need for me to ever be nervous about expressing myself publicly, when in actuality it's my story and I should own it. I know that sounds simple to say, but it has not been an easy task for me. It still remains my greatest challenge every time I present publicly.

I remember one friend sharing how she copes with the stress of public speaking. Indirectly, she masks her feelings through a character. She said that she just goes into character and speaks as though the audience is part of her production. She called it her way of masking her fears and insecurities so that no one knows her level of discomfort. That was the first time that I had ever heard someone articulate a strategy of masking when it came to public speaking. I became curious wanting to know more and to see if her technique could work to my advantage. What I've found is that we as human beings are a very complex species, with many layers of unresolved issues that stem from our childhood. We have many facets of who we are, and none of us are linear. We come with a plethora of issues, conditions, and circumstances that shape our thoughts and behaviors. In so many words, we become masters of masking our innermost feelings. We inevitably learn good and bad techniques of coping through our dilemmas. Publicly, we look and sound alike. The thing that makes us different from the other is how we truly feel about ourselves. This goes back to some of our core values, as in honesty, truth, and love of self. If folks do not understand their core values, then masking is the technique that they've mastered to get by. Therefore, you may never get to know the true person because masking has enabled them to make statements. It's not that they believe what they're saying is true, but instead what the majority is expecting them to say.

From the studies that I've done, I found that we mask as a technique for fear of exposing our vulnerabilities to others. We feel that we would be giving up control of our emotions to someone else should we reveal any form of weakness. With this ideology surrounding masking, men and women process things differently. Both sexes are trained from early on how masking is an acceptable technique for living. Think about it. A jovial boy runs and plays hard, falls and bruises his leg. Just as he's about to express his natural response to pain, his mother comes over to soothe his emotional needs while addressing his physical pain. A father, on the other hand, will tell his son to get up and brush it off. How many times have you have heard *"real men don't cry?"* This mindset is sickening to me because first and foremost it's a lie. Secondly, a child is not a man. To impose our own idiosyncrasies on that child will only reinforce that masking his pain away is an acceptable way of dealing with it.

In the previous example, women do not have to worry about the masculinity compromises that men are ridiculed for whenever they express themselves emotionally. Women on the other hand are taught as little girls that it's acceptable being outwardly emotional and they need not mask their feelings away. However, the challenges that they face are that they tend to be overly judged with insults of being too sensitive. I've seen instances in one of my past relationships where I was guilty of being insensitive to the needs of my mate. I was paralyzed in my actions to support her while she was experiencing some emotional challenges. As I recall, my emotional immaturity convinced me that she had the problem and not I. Avoidance was my approach towards her. Instead of accepting her with the dilemma that she was facing at the time, I wrongfully judged her for being a fragile human.

My selfishness could not see that her bruises were only for a moment.

Psychiatrist Karyn Hall suggested in her studies that people use different types of masks which act as *"a natural response to do whatever works to avoid the pain of believing others have judged, rejected or left you out."* There's no shame with admitting that I used several of her described masking techniques for coping, because most people use some form of masking as a way of dealing with life's daily responsibilities. In the example with my ex, I used the Avoidance Mask because I sought to avoid dealing with any and all pain. I didn't want to show emotional weakness to her because it made me feel vulnerable. What I unfortunately realized was that I spent so much time overly compensating for my weaknesses that I could not show consideration for another's weak moment. Over time, my poor coping skills lead me to the place where I no longer was concerned with how to live honest and free with open emotional expressions. Instead, I ended up learning how to function in this world just to protect and hide my vulnerabilities. While the Functional Masking is something that we all do and need, it's worse when you add poor coping skills to the equation.

As a business owner and leader in the community, I used the Functional Mask technique daily. One may say that this is probably the most commonly used mask. If you were to think about it, how could one be a successful leader if they did not know how to mask and categorize their feelings and occurrences that may influence the outcomes of an event? I'm quickly reminded of an early Thursday morning phone call that I received 4 years ago. My eldest brother drove for my limousine company. He and his coworker were scheduled to perform chauffeur duties for some clients that they had previously dropped off a week earlier on a cruise ship.

The hour was early and the day was cold when my brother's alarmed coworker called to inform me that my brother was bleeding through his nose and not responding to any verbal commands. By the tone of his voice, I began to ask him basic questions as whether or not he called 911. To my surprise, he informed me that he didn't call them and his second concern was who was going to drop off the customers to their homes, who were in the limousine that my brother was driving. Partially in disbelief by the information that he shared, I realized that I needed to mask my pain and fear in order to control a better outcome considering the circumstances.

When I arrived at the scene, I had to mask my feelings of fear and pain. I categorized my priorities based on the most important thing at the time. I learned that my brother had a massive heart attack behind the wheel. In spite of how I felt about seeing my brother laid out unconscious on the stretcher, there was absolutely nothing that I could do for him medically. Therefore, I left that responsibility to the 1st responders who were on scene. Secondly, my clients had to be reassured that things were going to work out and that they would get to their respective residences safely, in spite of what they just witnessed. Should I dare mention that the other driver was nowhere to be seen once I got on the scene. It took all that was in me not to lose my temper as I rehearsed his repeated lines in my head which were *"who is going to move the limo out of the street and take it back to the lot?"* I quickly realized that he was in a state of shock himself after seeing his friend/coworker dying before his eyes.

It was my Functional Mask that I wore because it was a temporary covering that shielded me from showing my internal emotional struggles. There's nothing good that I can surmise when you're forced to watch your brother fight for his life and you are powerless to do anything about it. This was by far one of the most difficult circumstances that one could ever imagine. I had to maintain control of my emotions and manage most of the controllable factors in the environment while keeping my customers and staff's emotions from escalating. In this example of masking, it doesn't have a negative connotation. In fact, because it is temporary, it is a healthier way of sustaining the emotional state of an uncontrolled environment. Needless to say, the customers made it to their respective destinations; I was able to return the damaged limousine back to our company's lot; and then join my brother and the medical team in the emergency room where he would perish within 45 minutes of being there.

In general, Dr. Karyn Hall further suggests that wearing a mask is *"a way of disappearing-being invisible."* It's not all together a bad thing. While there are other faces/masks that we wear to protect our emotions, we must caution ourselves because if someone wears masks too long, they may forget the very basic of human communal needs. She says, *"Avoiding feelings means you lose a part of who you are and increases the likelihood that you'll be depressed or anxious."* In fact, I've been diagnosed and treated over the years for clinical depression. It didn't surprise me to find that a large part of my coping skills are similar to those that Dr. Hall has outlined in her periodical *"Wearing Masks."* I know for certain that I've used her Avoidance, Functional, People Pleaser,

Anger and Happy Masks to shield my emotions during times of uncertainty. Furthermore, if I used them as techniques for coping, I'm sure that most if not all of us at some point in our walk use them daily.

I'm reminded of two separate examples where powerful political figures used their masking techniques differently while making important decisions for this nation. The first that comes to mind is President Barack H. Obama's choice to use lethal force to kill the Islamic Sect Leader Osama bin Laden. While the President was at the Annual Correspondent's Dinner delivering a speech full of political satire and jokes, his Military Cabinet Officials were underway in the final preparations to assassinate Osama bin Laden. President Obama did not show any signs that would have anyone to believe that he was uncomfortable with sending 2 Navy Seal Teams across the dangerous borders of Pakistan. In fact, even when one of the comics at the dinner made a joke about Osama bin Laden, the President continued to laugh and smile. It is in his ability to effectively use a masking technique to execute a life changing experience that would forever change the course of World History.

The second example of a powerful political figure who wears masks daily can be seen in our nation's present President,

Donald J. Trump. President Trump is known for waffling on issues as well as his mean-spirited sentiments towards individuals. Because he uses the negative attributes of masking, he keeps people at a distance. Even those in his Cabinet and closest to him are not sure what his stance is on issues. One day he'll speak about how he thinks NATO is obsolete; China's trade policies are horrible and that they rape our economy; and that we're probably better off with Syria's President Assad as the leader. When confronted by questions from the free press, he resorts to using the Anger Mask. Dr. Karyn Hall suggests that people who use the *Anger Mask* to keep people away from seeing them vulnerable. *"Anger feels more powerful than hurt, fear or sadness."* Through this theory, she equates angry people use this mask like the *"sheep dressed in porcupine quills."*

In spite of the many examples of individuals who use masking as a way of functioning, I still had to develop my own techniques. I needed to mask my feelings, so that I could become an effective public speaker. After reading more books, listening to audio recordings, as well as watching every YouTube video on masking, I devised a strategy. The first thing that I would do is get to the location early. This would give me a sense of familiarity with the area where I'll be speaking from. I would then rehearse my key points of discussion in my head. By the time I was ready to present, it was more about me speaking from a rehearsed script, than any interactions from the audience that would require a personal response. Finally, I'd make sure to move my eyes in a scanning direction through the audience without focusing on any one person. This reduced me from establishing a personal connection with anyone in the audience. This has become my foundation for public speaking.

Once I've established my groundwork for sharing, I then used my newly formed strategy that I call *"Shared Vulnerabilities."* In it, I deliberately raise an open-ended question to my audience, hence the title of this book, *"What's In Your Bag?"* While the title may seem catchy, it is purposed to get the audience thinking introspectively. It's also geared at getting folks to put their guards down once they realize that the room where we're gathered is a safe haven for them to express themselves openly, for at least the next 2 to 3 hours. We all have something in our bag of goodies that we're internally carry that may be corrosive to our very fabric or could even be a blessing to us. While the items in my bag may have once focused on the lack of self-worth, value and esteem, someone else may have other things in their bag of goodies. I recognize that our subconscious approach to masking tends to hide our vulnerable sides, preventing any of us to live honestly, openly and free.

When I first started presenting from the subject matter of *"What's In Your Bag,"* I couldn't help but look at the many items that I carry with me daily. The first of which was fear of public speaking. I wondered why I couldn't explain the fear and issues that I had with presenting before crowds. Occasionally I would get a flashback of my childhood. I would see myself as this 6-year-old boy who was just standing in front of the church during one of our Sunday School Easter Recitals. I stood front and center at the microphone just quivering, crying my heart out, and looking down at my feet. The reason behind my fears, I could never explain because I knew all of the people assembled before me. They were my family members, folks whose homes I'm sure I ate in or cousins that I played with. I couldn't explain it if I tried. What I do know is that my fears paralyzed me to the point that my lips would not part with words. Sometimes those fears still haunt me. It's as though my shy little boy named "Mickey" kept making his impromptu visits.

In spite of my fear of public speaking, I am now being called to speak before the masses. That is why the topic of fear is much of the focus of this chapter on wearing masks as a way of coping. By addressing my fear, I can get to the root of my apprehensions with public speaking. The more that I spoke, the more I realized I never truly addressed why I still carried these unexplainable fears. My voice would shake as though my life was on the line. I would perspire as if I just completed a marathon. It wasn't until I was pulled to the side by a friend of mine who had just heard me speak. I asked if everything was alright with my message. Did they get it? She responded, *"Yes, we got it. That's why I'm concerned about you."* Of course, that startled me because she caught me off guard. She went on to say that I did a great job and the people felt my sincerity. She then asked, *"What's wrong with you?"* I knew exactly what she meant by initiating the dialogue. Therefore, I just told her that I was under the weather, with the hopes that would pacify her inquiry. I was embarrassed to know that someone knew my limitations and fears.

Later in the week she asked me to meet her at a local eatery. I was a little hesitant on accepting her invitation, but I knew sooner or later I had to talk through my fears. She, on the other hand, is a public figure who weekly speaks to countless folks. Even though I knew she was a pro at this thing, I didn't want her to see my weakness because she saw me as this all-knowing person; a wise man to be exact. She depended on my knowledge and expertise for solving the issues that she faced. Therefore, I had many reservations in sharing my vulnerabilities with her. I agreed to meet with her at Panera Bread to talk. I figured that in that type of environment with food and strange folks, most of the conversation wouldn't get so heavy. Once we got past the passive gestures of meeting, she went all the way on me. *"You weren't sick and don't give me that bull crap. You were nervous as heck."* I took a moment to catch myself. Normally I'm pretty good with quick responses, but this one had me once again paralyzed. As quietness engulfed my presence, tears began to form in the corners of my eyes. Before I realized, she was passing me a tissue.

I wasn't tearing because of something that she said. I was tearing because I never admitted to another about my fears. She was the first person that felt compelled to help me conquer my fear of public speaking. Just as this may have been the catalyst for me conquering my fear, it never truly resolved anything. During our discussion, she taught me her method for masking her anxieties by focusing on other things. What she taught was that it mattered not what causes me to tremble, what mattered most to her was how to make it past that minute to the next. In as much as I appreciated how she helped me with her approach, I was more disappointed that she was never curious about what troubled me.

She sought to comfort me by telling me that she too struggled at times with anxiety before speaking publicly. She said that whenever her anxiety peaked, she would sip from a cup of water that she previously placed at the podium as a way of distracting herself from what was going on inside her head. Immediately I realized what she was saying because I always watched "Live with *Kelly and Mike TV Show*" in the mornings. I noticed that whenever Michael Strahan struggled with masking his personal feelings, he too would sip from a mug and drink, at least that is what I initially thought. After a closer look at him, I realized that in most cases he would only put the cup to his mouth but never drink. I then thought about every comedian that's on stage, who also sips and quenches their imaginary thirst. It wasn't long from that moment that I began to pensively stare at everyone who was eating around us. I watched to see if they were really drinking or sipping. I know, you're probably thinking that I'm a little touched because I'm paying attention to small details. At this stage, I'm more concerned with identifying what causes me to mask those traits that I have that make me uneasy about being able to share my vulnerabilities.

In spite of it all, I am grateful to my friend for having the courage to confront me on my issues. Not often will you find a friend who is willing to protect your vulnerabilities while also helping you to identify with your flaws. My takeaway from her is to just mask everything as long as you don't break in front of the people. Her theory forced me to further conclude that if she's a successful public figure and can only suggest masking, then she too is haunted by her child within. Her approach can only make me wonder *if I was the only one who has a little child who peeks out his/her little head wanting to be seen?* I started looking at everyone that I knew differently. I studied their behavior and looked at how they reacted to things. I was happy to conclude that I was not alone.

One day I received a call from the wife of a very dear friend of mine who wanted me to meet up with her. She knew how much I loved her and her husband. If truth be told, I looked up to them as a power couple. On the surface, he was a father of 3 beautiful girls, all of college age; and a devoted husband who went home every night to the same woman, his wife. Never in the time that I've known him did I ever have any knowledge of him straying from his family. He had a very successful career, making 6 figures easily. From my bird's eye view, he had it all. It wasn't until this one evening of hanging out with him that I realized that he had a serious drinking problem. Together we drank but never once did I count how many drinks he ingested. It took two years before I realized that he was always at the bar before me and remained there after I left. It was his wife who one day found me and bent my ear with her stories of a troubled man. I couldn't for the life in me believe all that she was saying.

As she spoke, she started expressing the many years of his inability to bring his drinking under control. In all honesty, I truly didn't want to hear what she had to say. She started telling me about how he was verbally abusive, and at times violent against her and the girls. Unable to keep my cool, I asked her if he was the way she was describing him then, why didn't she just leave. She then told me that she couldn't. She said that they had built a very successful lifestyle and didn't want to lose all that they established. Noticing my awkward silence, tears began to form in the corners of her eyes. She began to justify her staying as though she had something to prove to me. The more she spoke, the more and more I got disturbed listening to her. In all that she said, she never once stated love was the reason she stayed in the relationship. Never once did love ever part her lips. It occurred to me that she sold her soul for the sake of having a successful image in the public eye. How important does her value as a woman come into effect when she's so freely willing to compromise so much of herself for so little?

She went as far as to tell me about her father being an alcoholic and how her mother stood by his side. There was no need for her to put it all on the line. Before long, I looked down at my watch only to realize that she and I had been speaking for nearly 2 hours. I interrupted her with the question of *"Why are you telling me this now? Why are you speaking so strongly about my friend?"* In a shaky voice and tears in her eyes, she explained how they were out one night having a good time. They went to a retirement party of one of her former colleagues. She said that he really didn't want to attend. He only went to keep her company. As she continued speaking, she got more and more emotional. Unsure as to the cause of her deep emotions, I grabbed her and asked what's wrong? Tell me what's going on. She proceeded to tell me that my childhood friend was in the hospital in critical condition. He was barely holding on to life. She said that they had a car accident while leaving her friend's party. Shocked with my mouth wide open, she continued crying and talking, talking and crying until her emotions got the best of her. Sobbing in my arms, I held her.

Later on that day, I went to the hospital to see how he was improving. Just watching the respirator initiate his breaths, I began to hold mine. I began to hyperventilate. His attending nurse came to my side asking me if I needed help. I could only tell her that I was his friend and was just in my emotions at the time. She began to tell me how lucky he was because the alcohol level in his blood had reached lethal limits. I couldn't help but ask her about the bandages around his head. She began to tell me how he suffered some brain swelling, a fractured pelvis, 2 broken ribs and a collapsed lung from the impact of his car running into the wall. I asked her if he was the only one injured. She informed me that the other driver that he hit was moved out of critical care and is now in stable condition. I sighed with relief.

While watching my friend fight for his life, my mind took me back to our childhood when we both were young and innocent. We played marbles, checkers, and raced up and down the streets. We ran with so much vigor that we didn't have a care in the world. His parents were like parents to me. We were so close that we just as well could have been brothers. I could only try and find where he and I went wrong. Where did our paths differ; and why? Upon leaving his bedside, I was determined to understand his emotional pathology and what could have possibly lead him to using alcohol as a crutch. I couldn't help but think that if alcohol was his vice, then we all must have something. I can only hope that he recovers and no one dies as a result of his actions.

Let me be the first to say that I'm not perfect. Actually, I'm a flawed individual with complex issues. There's nothing simple about my life story. I never want you to get the impression that I'm judging my friends or the Presidents of the United States. I only want you to know that in the case of my friend, I'm sure he knows the ramification of what alcoholism can lead to. I'm sure he advises his 3 daughters not to drink and drive. I'm sure he doesn't even look at himself as an alcoholic. He believes in God and is a Deacon at his local church. So many of our issues lead to bad habits, which in his case has become an addiction. It is in the addiction, that we slowly become addicted to making bad choices for ourselves. As long as we're successful at masking issues, what else should matter?

What Mask Are You Wearing? Ah!

UNPACKING ONE ITEM AT A TIME

You are responsible for your life.
You can't keep blaming somebody else for
Your dysfunction. Life is really about moving on.

Oprah Winfrey

UNPACKING ONE ITEM AT A TIME

CHAPTER 7

EMBRACING CHANGE

Often, I think about the beauty of Fall; the warmth of Summer; the new birth of Spring; and the quiet majestic chill of Winter. With each passing season, I spend a lot of time enjoying all of the attributes that each one possesses. The beauty that I find in these seasons, is that while I'm in full merriment with one, I can still hope and look forward to enjoying the possibilities of the next, without compromising the blessings of the season that I'm experiencing. This is how I've come to accept life. Life, with its many ups and downs, is like the interchanging seasons of time.

As a child, Winter was my favorite time of the year. I believe it was mainly due to the majestic feelings of purity that the white snow afforded me. For the first time in the year, I no longer had to see the shattered glass littered pavements outside my doorstep. The snow added beauty to the abandoned shacks and fragmented frames that were shells of buildings that were destroyed by the previous summer flames. Our vacant lots of overgrown weeds and trails of despair, were now beautiful picturesque landscapes that went on for miles. Those things that the snow couldn't cover became the season's monuments, frozen in time. It was winter that made me dream of a heaven that was told to me as my nightly bedtime stories. There, I would walk freely through the heavens on its huge, beautiful, white, robust clouds. From those clouds, fell crystals of snow to the earth.

Despite the season's low temperatures, my friends and I would take to our backyards and local parks, sliding down the white covered mounds of debris. We'd ride our bikes for hours through the snow, as if our tires were plows and the cold weather was a fragment of our imagination. We'd take to the ice as if we were those professional ice skaters that we saw on our television screens, who glided around the Rockefeller Center's ice skating rink. I even remember skating with my ugly big toed jeepers, hoping to wear an even bigger hole in them. I hated those sneakers that my Mom forced me to wear. Those memories seem as though they were yesterday. I still smile at just the thought. As I write this chapter, I'm in my winter season of life. It's not only about the majestic beauty of the snow or the endless nights of summer. It's more about the possibility that change offers me, as well as each and every one of us, should we be willing to engage it.

Have you ever had problems that exhausted and weighed you down to the point of giving up? It's in those seasons of strife and challenge that we must seek change as a positive antidote to altering the trajectory of our circumstances. Far too often, we allow our fears, levels of discomfort, and the lull of complacency to keep us frozen from our pursuit of happiness and success. In another chapter of this book, I referenced change as a key component in achieving success. We must become willing participants in the process of change should we truly desire success, even if it causes levels of discomfort. How can you expect to reach your destination if you're not willing to change from where you are?

Change is a process that requires action. It's not an event or occasion. It's the process that leads to the result. Whether it's temporary or permanent, we must be willing to engage the process if we expect to have different outcomes. Sometimes when I speak before an audience about my experiences in business, I'm asked the question of *how did I achieve the goals that I've set for myself*. I tell folks everywhere that change begins with a thought, an alternate approach to the way we see things. Sometimes we make things more complicated than they really are. We overthink, underestimate, and at times get overwhelmed with fears of the unknown. It becomes these barriers that impede our desire to proceed. We must remember that we have to give ourselves more credit, and trust our inner voice a lot more than we do. We must also recognize the impulses of change as they enter our mind and trigger our thought process. In addition, we must have a willingness to transform our thoughts into action. That's the part that takes work.

Change can sometimes be painful. I often reference comedian Steve Harvey when I speak about the obstacles that I've encountered before I succeeded reaching some of my goals. He uses the analogy of jumping off a cliff as a way of motivating people to engage change. He's not suggesting by any means, that people jump to their deaths. It's to the contrary. He warns them metaphorically that you may hit some rocks on the way down and get a few bruises on your backside. He lets them know that pain may be part of the process of the jump. He then promises you that two things will happen if you are willing to take *the jump*. After listening to his story, I've surmised that there are actually three things that occur when you take the jump.

The first and most important thing that occurs when you decide to take the jump is that you become an agent of change. You've decided to transform your thoughts into actions. Whether or not it works in your favor is secondary to the fact that you initiated change. Secondly, Harvey promises that your parachute will not open right away. This is the time when you get those bumps and bruises. It's when change provokes you in a way that your fears and obstacles force you to second guess your decisions. Even with these obstacles present, they must be accepted as part of the process. I'm reminded of a principle that Joyce Meyer often speaks of. She suggests that if it's fear that keeps you bound from moving forward in life, then *do it afraid*. I, along with Harvey and Meyer agree that fear is a given that you must acknowledge, but not allow it to stop you from reaching your goal.

When Harvey says that the parachute may not open right away, I'm reminded of the fears that I had when I decided to close a few of my companies. I was at crossroad in my life. Do I continue as I'm doing by working with no gratification, or do I pursue the calling that God placed on my life? I knew that if I wanted more, my path had to change. I had to choose to embrace and become a participant in the process of change. Prior to making the decision to pursue a different path, I became accustomed to a certain dollar and lifestyle. By me choosing this new career path, the process of change turned my finances upside down. My bills began to mount as my revenue stream dwindled. Due to the fact that I never lived above my means, I was able to still maintain a sense of self and value. I experienced my harshest financial realities of not having the same financial cushions. In spite of the bumps and bruises, I continued on my path of change. That's when I called the airline and made my reservation to jump.

Considering Harvey's example of jumping off of a cliff and the fact that my niece took a parachuting class a few months prior, I chose to jump and experience firsthand what a free-falling jump would feel like. I used his metaphor of conquering your fears as one of my motivating factors in conquering my fears and frustrations with life. Once I made my reservation and boarded the small Cessna plane, I, along with 6 others were instructed to sit low and follow the instructions of the lead jumper. There I sat trying to pay attention to every word he was giving, but my emotions got the best of me. I couldn't help from thinking about the possibilities that my parachute just may not open. I began to think about my Mom and how she would feel knowing that her baby died doing what he wanted verses battling his daily feelings of living unfulfilled. I also began to think about my remaining businesses and how my employees would survive without me. For some reason my Amway tag line kept hitting my spirit. I heard over and over, *"People don't plan to fail. They fail to plan."* I began to think if what I was about to do was part of God's plan for me, or was it me for once living free and without a plan? With all of those rushing thoughts, I found peace in knowing that no matter what, it would soon be over.

The jump was more than just the typical recreational jump as seen by others. It was a place for me to carry all my emotional and spiritual burdens high into the heavens and throw them out to the Lord. In some strange way, I felt like I finally was going to totally trust in Him. As the plane reached its maximum height, the pilot tipped it slightly to the right, forcing me to fall out of the door. Despite my fear of heights and the uncertainties before my life, I took to the skies full of emotions. Not realizing all that I was to gain from the jump, I felt rewarded because I chose to embrace the needed changes in my life. I knew that the first change had to begin with my mind. The fact that I put my thoughts into action made me feel that I no longer had to tackle my battles alone.

During the fall, I envisioned myself as a child, flying freely above all of my problems. It wasn't that they no longer existed, it was just I was able to step away and look at them from a different perspective. The first part of the fall was my fear phase. I had absolutely no control of my existence or where I was going. There was no way that I could convert my actions back to my thoughts of change. The only thing that I saw was a guaranteed meeting with the ground, and it was fast approaching. While in the free fall, I heard businesswoman/motivational speaker Lisa Nichols say, *"Everything that I need to get back up, I have in me."* It seemed like once I heard those words, I then saw the Lord as my parachute and I knew that He had me covered. Upon the chute's opening, I felt a sense of peace that surpassed all understanding. I could not put it all into words the joy that I got when I began to soar and glide above all of my circumstances. The gliding enabled me to breath while still in life's fight. I was now experiencing what it means to trust Him. God reminded me that I was in a controlled glide. From that viewpoint, I selected which of my problems I was going to land on first.

Finally, Harvey promises that if you do not jump, or as I would like to say engage in change, *"Your parachute will never open."* This is how most of us live our lives, very cautiously. In as much as we would like to move into that next season of our life's journey, we restrict ourselves. We live within the confines of our fears with hopes of miraculous changes. We want more out of life, but we are not willing to engage life through the acceptance of change. Life coach Catherine Pratt suggests that there are 6 basic reasons why people are afraid of change. She believes that people fear the unknown; doubt themselves; isolate themselves and agonize over decisions; forget that there's always an option; focus on the external benchmarks and less on emotional needs; and finally, they handcuff themselves to those external benchmarks.

While Pratt's study may show why people fear change, all of her reasons did not apply to me because decision making wasn't one of my fears. In fact, I didn't spend much time agonizing over making decisions because I knew that I was never going to step out on my own. Part of my fear with change was due to my low self-esteem. It imprisoned me to the point that I lacked self-worth and confidence. Even though I knew I possessed the ability to do almost anything, my lack of confidence wouldn't enable me to hurdle my emotional dilemmas at the time. Because of that, I truly felt that I wasn't prepared for the world that was before me. I was shy, bashful, and at times too timid to raise my voice in front of people. I was attached to my insecurities and everything else that would not allow me the comforts of freedom. Having an extraverted brother who he and I were reared as though we were twins didn't help the matter either. He was very outspoken and longed for attention. I, on the other hand, chose to retreat and hide behind his voice. Unfortunately, me taking that position did two things. It falsely empowered him, reinforcing that his behavior and actions were right and acceptable by me. Secondly, by voluntarily giving up my power to him, I forbade myself the right to have individual thoughts.

Aside from the sense of security that my brother afforded me, I found some comfort in the church when it came to speaking out. There, I was able to function freely, especially from believing that I needed my brother's approval. There my insecurities were secondary. I remember one day I was determined to step out of my comfort zone and ask one of the elders for some advice. By the time I built up enough confidence to ask for what I wanted, they told me to pray, have faith, then watch the Lord deliver. I wasn't ready for that response because I was more focused on them hearing me speak than anything else. So, I took their advice. I opened my Bible. Not only did the Lord not deliver what I prayed for, I learned the hard way that faith and prayer weren't enough to fulfill my wishes. I had to be persistent and put in some work. I began to read to ensure that I understood what was written in the *Book of James Chapter 2, Verse 24: You see that a person is considered righteous by what they do and not by faith alone.* From that, I got a better understanding that faith and prayer will get me to a point, but it's the additional ingredients of my actions and work that will get me to the next season.

This reminds me of a former athlete and ESPN Analyst Jay Williams and the hard work that it took for him to get to the next season in life. Recently he's been featured on many radio and talk shows. I was drawn to him through one of Oprah Winfrey's Super Soul Sunday shows, under the topic of *"Letting go to find himself."* There he expounded on his tribulation and triumphs. I was curious with how he viewed the concept of change considering his near death experience. Realizing that maybe he was dealt a bad hand in life, he chose to accept the hand he was given, and play it to the best of his abilities. I was amazed to hear him speak from a viewpoint of accepting life. He used that experience to write and publish his book entitled, *"Life Is Not An Accident."*

Here, Jay Williams story shows how change can bring about times of inconvenience. By definition, inconvenience is the cause of trouble, difficulties, or discomfort. Its synonyms are unfortunate, unfavorable, irritating, difficult, awkward, problematic, worrisome and distressing to name a few. Often, when using the word inconvenient, we associate it with having a negative connotation. The thing that I find interesting about inconvenience is that though by definition its attributes are difficulties and discomfort, it can also lead to positive results. In the case of Jay Williams, he was the top pick for the NBA's selection of collegiate athletes. He was chosen by the Chicago Bulls for the position of point guard and paid handsomely for his potential. One day after leaving a meeting, he had a horrible motorcycle accident that almost ended his life, but definitely ended his career as a professional basketball player. With over ten surgeries, nerve damage, and an addiction to prescription drugs, he knew that his recovery would be difficult. In spite of the many bone breaks, his biggest challenge came from his mental injuries. It would take all of his trials to realize that he had to retrain and rethink how he viewed and lived his life. With all odds stacked against him, he was able to move into his next season in life and carve out a new career once he recovered from the accident. I must say that Williams embraced his change and saw the opportunity within a chaotic situation.

How many times have you been placed in a situation where drastic changes have forced you to reconsider how you live your life? I know I have. Because of those situations, I have a better understanding of what this older gentleman has been telling me all of my life. He said, *you have to go through the rain in order to see the sunshine*. Sometimes the visions that we have for ourselves are not clearly carved into our purpose driven lives. If our purpose negates our sacrifice, would we then see the opportunity to grow by embracing change? We get stuck in our seasons of hope, wants, and desires, and very seldom proceed to our season of promises. I say that it is a must that we embrace life on its terms because change is the one constant thing or event that we can be certain of. Everything must change.

I'm reminded of the relationship that I have with myself and others. I use to wonder if I would be willing or had the confidence to change course and walk away from a bad relationship. That makes me raise the question, *has the inconvenience of change forced you to stay in relationships that you know have long past their season of fertility?* I'm not solely referring to a relationship with a mate. I'm referring to any relationship with another person that was no longer producing positive fruit of emotional growth. Might you have stayed solely because familiarity was more comfortable than the uncertainties of change? Even though change may promote fears of uncertainty, it does not equate to being lonely. Many of us wrestle with fears of loneliness that we accept complacency, and at times neglect and abuse as normal. How often have you heard someone say *I don't want to be alone?* What I've come to accept is that it's okay for me to be alone because it does not mean that I'm lonely. What it means is I've consciously taken the position to view change with optimism.

The mere fact that someone knows the relationship that they are in is toxic, is secondary to their willingness to embrace change by leaving it. We all possess the ability to change, but not all are willing to confront the attributes of change head on. Many folks who are in relationships that appear healthy are in fact lonely. The mindset of that person in the toxic relationship may feel it's more comforting having someone to hold and talk to, instead of them having to hear the echoes of an empty room. They can also be the product of abuse and feel helpless to leave. As previously mentioned, change promotes fears of the unknown, *being is easier than becoming*. More often than not, we become complacent in the conditions that we're in. We lack the confidence in knowing that we already have what it takes to endure the inconveniences that may come with change. I've heard folks say that they're just not emotionally ready to commit to the sacrifices needed to grow. My heart aches for them.

Sometimes it's easier for me to hear others as they share their struggles with the inconveniences of change, than it is for me to share. I admit to have battled similar issues. Mine did not center on an intimate relationship with a woman. Many of my struggles were primarily focused on either my weight or some of my business relationships. If I take this moment to talk about my battles with my weight, I'll go on and on. What I'm willing to admit about it is that the phrase *big boned* is a figuratively used phrase with no literal meaning. For the longest I justified keeping some associates near for the sole purpose of my convenience. I knew that the termination of those relationships would bring on high levels of stress that I wasn't ready to take on. In order to justify things, I would question myself, *who would do the job? Why can't someone else go there?* As selfish as those statements may sound, it was the life and thought process that I once possessed. If that wasn't enough, sometimes my ego got in the way. *What would they think of me if they saw me doing that job?* However, entitled that may sound, I kept expired relationships close to me. Their presence fostered a false sense of security that justified me not having to face change alone. I was too weak within myself to face the burdens and responsibilities that came with change.

When I finally thought that I positioned myself in a place of readiness for embracing the changes that I sought, I realized that change required me to work. I had to work hard at completing each and every new task that arose. My biggest challenge came when I had to see hope and promise in a decision I made that didn't yield immediate tangible results. The hardships of closing companies, considering bankruptcy, and laying off employees were the biproducts of the choices that I made. There was no immediate reward in closing those businesses. I fell backwards, spiraling into old and newly resurrected struggles of depression, and at times contemplated suicide. I constantly had to dig deep and remind myself that the choice to induce change at this point in my journey was the right decision. My ability to rise to the occasion and identify my purpose through the rubble, affirmed in me that I made the right choice.

Recently I engaged various people on the topic of change because of what I went through. Knowing that change is inevitable, I wanted to know how it impacted them. Sometimes we prematurely make major life changes. We rush into decisions without considering the probable outcomes. In most cases, rushed decisions often yield unfavorable results. My choice to close some of my companies wasn't a rushed decision. I just didn't have an inkling as to what I would be forced to face based on my decision. The most profound impact that change had on me was that I was forced to view my life and death differently. No one ever told me that each of the companies that I closed would be like burying a child, especially since I didn't have children of my own. I didn't realize that there was an emotional connection that I had with my companies, from their births, watching them prosper, and now consciously leading them to their demise. The impact of that change affected me emotionally despite the fact that I knew that I had God's favor all around me. It forced me to suggest to others that before they consider changing their careers, lifestyles, and family structures, remember to take the needed time to plan their futures.

As I think about change, death has to be the one major event that affects us all. Recently, I went through a season with the deaths of five of my dear loved ones. With each one of them, I had a different relationship. I found myself experiencing a plethora of emotions, none of which were the same. It wasn't until I grieved the loss of one of my closest childhood friends that I began to question whether or not death was an inconvenience. I didn't solely question it from the selfish perspective of me having to live without his presence. I first began to question it when he raised the issue. Before you start to wonder, I ask that you not question or doubt our faith in God because we both are firm believers in Christ. The way in which people correlate death with inconvenience is relative to each of their own perspectives. I'm quickly reminded that even when Yeshua "Jesus" was slew to the tree, he questioned his father saying, *"Eloi, Eloi, lama sabachani?"* translated meaning, "My God, My God, why have thou forsaken me? Therefore, I've surmised that it is human to question the timing and inconvenience of death.

When I look at my friend's life, he was in the midst of three major directorial projects, one of which was with me. He was a devoted father, proud grandfather, present son, and dear friend to many. He was a noted professor at a prestigious university where he ensured that people of color would have an opportunity to study there and abroad. He owned his own production company and employed six individuals whose livelihoods depended on his wellbeing. He ensured that his production narratives were written, told, and produced by those affected. He was a man on a mission. From the time that he was hospitalized, up until two days before receiving his diagnosis, we spoke about his commitment to the children. We laughed at getting old and reminisced about how we were going to be two old men in rockers, giving counsel to the up and coming generation of directors and actors. We spoke in the affirmative and accepted aging, aches, and even death as part of the season of life that we were venturing in to. Never once did we in those moments question the concept that death was an inconvenience because the hopes of a prosperous future was ahead of us. If I may take a moment and make a parallel to my friend's story, I will tell you about my brother. Four years ago, I lost my eldest brother at the age of 51. He was driving one of my limousines when he had a massive heart attack. If truth be told, I didn't mourn his loss in a way that I would question whether or not his death was an inconvenience to me. If I were to revisit that time and day, I may be able to support the position that death is inconvenient without feeling some kind of way about the negative connotations associated with it. I can look at the fact that I was awaken out of my sleep early in the morning by a frantic coworker. I can say that there were customers in the rear of the vehicle who needed to be taken home. Or maybe, I can say that my crashed limousine was left in the middle of the street, and it needed to be returned back to the lot. While all of those things can be used to support the position of the inconveniences of death, I didn't feel that way at all. Maybe, that was due to the fact that I had to compartmentalize my emotions in order to address all of the needs that were before me.

The interesting thing about death and inconvenience is how we define and assign it to our lives and circumstances. Both guys died within a relatively short time after their 50th birthdays, and God granted me the honor of seeing both within 8hrs. of their transitions. Based on our relationships and history of fellowship, none of us would have ever believed that this day would come as soon as it did. What I can say about both of these men is that they lived their last two years as though they knew that time was of the essence. My brother relocated back to New Jersey to be with his family. My dear friend traveled more and carried a heavier load than he had done previously. They both became very focused on living their best lives.

The thoughts of death being an inconvenience was planted in my head and spirit by my friend when he received his terminal diagnosis. The air of life was sucked out of his spirit. I remember my days sitting with him as he stared downward to the floor, as if he was watching his life play on a stage. Occasionally I'd get a chuckle out of him or the big smile that I longed to see. He began to question the inconvenience of death with *Why Lord, Why? I have so much more to do. Why now?* As the days went on, the depth of his silent contemplations began to get longer and longer. I tried the best that I could to hold back my emotions, even though it brought tears to my spirit. As the pressure of those moments continued to engulf me, I subtly wiped my tears away. It was then that I saw how inconvenient death was for him and at times, even me. This was the first time that I can truly say that I questioned God for taking a life.

I finally got to witness firsthand how inconvenient death was. It was inconvenient for him because that's how he felt when he realized that he didn't have the time to complete his tasks. He was forced to face his mortality in spite of the many daily responsibilities he had at his door. With all of the many shouts, cries, curses, frustrations, disappointments, and prayers that we shared, time waits for no one. I've come to accept that death may be inconvenient when there's an unforeseen obstacle before you that your human experience cannot hurdle while walking in your purpose. While some may argue that death is a part of all of our purposes, our human needs and experiences often leave us unfulfilled and yearning for more.

As I visited with my friend during his last days and final hours, I began to see a big difference in him. He began to embrace change. His spirit seemed resigned in peace. Though he was nearing his transition, he occasionally reminded us with a smile or scratch that he's yet alive. I thought about the story of Yeshua when he was asleep on a boat in the middle of the sea. A huge storm arose causing panic amongst His disciples. He wasn't awakened by the motion of the waves. He was awakened by his frantic disciples saying, "LORD, save us! We're going to drown!" Yeshua replied, "You of little faith, why are you so afraid?" He then stood up and faced the storm saying, "Peace be still." It was that kind of peace that I found while my friend laid there resting. While the world around him was somewhat chaotic, he continued to rest in the assurance that he embraced his change.

A person who never made a mistake
Never tried anything new.

Albert Einstein

UNPACKING ONE ITEM AT A TIME

CHAPTER 8

ACTS OF SERVICE

They should have given more! They have it to give! Can you remember a time when you thought someone should have given more? Whether it was a gift, fundraiser or even a church offering, it shouldn't matter to you how much someone else gives. Your concern should be about what you're doing for someone else and/or a greater cause. Far too often I've witnessed so many folks suggest the measure of someone else's gift. You would believe they had knowledge of that person's personal finances. I raise these concerns, not solely based on my philanthropic work, but on the lack of support and acts of service of so many others who have yet to yield from their capacities. Service should be a requirement for each and every able-bodied person.

This takes me to a conversation that I had with a very close friend of mine. She's a single parent of 3 beautiful children. Though she's been driving her ship solo as a single parent, never once have I ever heard her complain about the responsibilities of raising and being the sole provider for her family. In fact, she makes it a point to weekly save a portion of her earnings so that she can take her family on annual vacations to different parts of the country. I've always admired her hustle and determination. One day I asked her, *"What drives you?"* Without any hesitation, she replied, *"my mother always told us that when we have kids to do better by them.*

So, when I had my kids, I was determined to do more for mine." Her response did not surprise me based upon what I've learned about her.

In these few years of knowing her, I've watched as she taught her children the responsibility of saving and service. Just as she would sacrifice and save a portion of her pay, I listened to her tell me how she and the kids had different charities which they donate their money to. While listening to her, I realized that a large part of who we become in life is attributed to the behaviors that our parents display before us as children. Once again, I must reference psychologist John Bradshaw and his "Infancy Syndrome." Part of his philosophy speaks to us as just being older children who carry the same mess, love and pain from our childhood. He says that unless we're willing to address those past issues, we'll forever carry them with us to the future. How beautiful of a world would this be if we were all willing to deposit love, compassion, forgiveness and kind acts of service into the spirits and minds of our children? I was pleased to know that this mother was depositing and demonstrating to her children those values that I find to be so important.

My parents demonstrated many high-quality values including that of service before my siblings and I. Growing up in the inner city, I was always under the impression that we were poor. We didn't have the latest games and toys that hit the market. I didn't think that my parents were able to give us the desires of our heart as I thought my friends' parents did for them. What our parents did was ensured that we had a balance of responsibilities and recreation. When it came to acts of service, my parents would take us to our family church to shovel in the winter, clean the sanctuary, take out the garbage, help the senior community with odd jobs, assist the staff at the church's day care facility and we even laid tile on the basement floor. Just when I thought that we were poor, there were other families in our church who had less. I remember my parents making us gather up our old clothes into large Hefty plastic bags so that we could drop them off to other member's homes. Though I was too young to sum up our actions to be defined as service, what I got from the experience was a sense of satisfaction. I was happy to know that I was doing something good for someone else. I realized that it was my parents who planted the seed of giving to others in me. Yes, I give them the credit to my introductory experiences into the acts of service in which I've carried into my adulthood.

As I got a little older, my dad once told me how he admired my efforts when he found out that I was giving a portion of my earnings to the nonprofit organization "The Christian Children's Fund." In all honesty, I never thought that he noticed what I was doing. I was somewhat shy about letting anyone know. I truly believed that he might have said something negative to me, considering I was giving money to others instead of more to our household. It was to this organization, the Christian Children's Fund that I would proudly mail in my little $30 per month for the 2 kids that I sponsored. They would write me letters with their pictures attached. Though I was only 16 at the time and only had a part-time job at a local clothing store, I watched those commercials with much guilt, as they ran on my television screen asking for donations. I was proud to know that through this organization I had a daughter named Habwah, who lived in Kenya and a son Kutika from Uganda. I remember as though it was yesterday. I felt bad that many of those individuals that I saw on my television screen didn't have the basic necessities; a home, running water, or even food to eat. It seemed the older I got, the more I became appreciative for the little that I had.

It has become a part of my mission to recapture that portion of my childhood that inspired me the most. Little did I know that these same characteristics and initiatives that were displayed then, would continue into my adulthood. I am so grateful today for having an awareness and making a conscious decision to help our poor, disabled, and disenfranchised people of all ages, sexes, religions, colors and creeds with their needs. I realized a long time ago that there are always folks with greater needs than myself. In the poem written by Max Ehrmann entitled "Desiderata," the author mentioned this very basic point *"...If you compare yourself to others, you may become vain and bitter; for always there will be greater and lesser persons than yourself."* At the end of this piece he concludes with *"Strive to be happy."*

As I matured, happiness for me meant traveling abroad and searching for ways to improve the lives and conditions of others. One of the first places that I went was to the continent of Africa. I wanted to see where and how my dollars impacted others. If I were to say that I didn't see a difference in the look of the people I saw on the television screen as a kid, I'd be lying. I would equally be naive if I were to believe that it was because of my dollars that the population there looked different. What I believe to be certain is that the dollars which I and so many others sowed into the Christian Children's Fund account, collectively impacted the people of those communities and regions which they serviced.

It would be later that my naivety would teach me one of the hardest lessons in giving. I thought that other people respected and appreciated my acts of service. I wasn't prepared for the amount of criticism that I received as a result of sending money to an online organization. I was asked question after question like, *"Do you really think your money is going to reach those people? How do you know that those letters are genuine that have those kids faces on them? How do you know your money is really going towards the kids? How much of it actually goes to those kids that they're exploiting?"* Though I stood in my conviction of what service meant to me, initially the comments did trouble my spirit. It would take a while before my skin would harden to the criticism that so many gave as a result of me doing as I did. It was with the ridicule and sly remarks that I believed that has helped to shape my convictions in life.

Internally for the first time, I began to ask myself the same questions of why am I doing this as well as questioning the origin of the letters. Just as the questions came in, I realized that I had to follow my heart. Little did I know that those feelings from my heart which propelled me to give would later be defined as my "inner voice." As for those who continued to raise the questions about the validity of those letters and the organization, I too began to raise the level of my responses to them. I began to raise the brows of all who were willing to share their views. I would ask them, "Why not give?" I would then ask, "If it's your goal to discourage me from something that I enjoy doing, then what better option might you have for me?" Their lack of reasonable responses began to chill me. I froze in my tracks after realizing that I didn't have to defend the act of doing a good deed. Neither did I need to defend the Christian Children's Fund. I'm sure they have their own team of lawyers for that.

It has been through my "inner voice" that I chose to listen to when making decisions that impacted the lives of others. I could not help but to reflect on the blessings that I've received through the process of giving from my heart. In doing so, I began to get a better understanding of who I was becoming as a man. I started seeing my life's purpose blossom before me. What I came to realize was that the best gifts in life were not tangible items. They are the things that no one can ever assign a dollar value to; for material gains will last but for a time until its lure and attraction wears off. I get so much more out of giving, especially when I feel the love and see the results of my conscious choice to give. To see the innocence of a smile and the relief of a kind gesture, warms my heart. You know, I got it! It's in the process of giving and knowing that I'm making a positive impact in someone's life that I've gained the greater rewards.

community. It was my neighbors who were assembled on their porches at 1:20 a.m., playing a random card game of bid whist when they saw 2 strange men running from behind our home. Within 5 seconds of their disappearance, Carol, my neighbor blew that familiar neighborhood alarm screaming at the top of her lungs, *"fire, fire!"* Maybe it was those other neighbors who risked their lives by running into the fire in search of the 2 little girls who would later perish. The idea that lay folks who give of their capacities daily is refreshing to know and witness. For me it means that we all possess the philanthropic abilities of giving. Each of us have it within our own capacity to give so much more of ourselves than we actually give ourselves the credit for. It's not only through our finances that we show service, but also through our time and commitment. When we better the lives of others, we experience life's beauty in giving. The challenge that we face as a collective society is whether or not we're able to make the same connections of giving when we're not solely driven by emotions and adrenaline.

As we stood on the curb watching our life's history burn up in the flames, I couldn't help but notice those other heroes and *sheroes* who came to our aid. What seemed like seconds, I'm sure was really minutes before the fire department would arrive on the scene. Shortly after them, and I'm sure it was within an hour the Salvation Army and the American Red Cross trucks sped down the street. They too came to provide us with the support and aid that we needed. I saw them off to the side giving out blankets to my parents and fellow fire victims; water and beverages to the fire and police officers; and little bites of snacks to nibble on to keep us nourished. It was my neighbor who stood in height inches over me who would run in his house and give me a pair of his sweat socks to cover my bare feet. I'm not sure he knew how much his kind gesture impacted my life. We had to wait for hours to see the remnants that the fire left as the firemen carried the 2 nonresponsive bodies out of the house in body bags. Lost without a home, the American Red Cross provided us and those who needed it with immediate shelter. They gave us coupons to the Lincoln Motel, a local welfare hotel where we could rest from the elements and hopefully find some sense of understanding to what just occurred. Without their support, I'm not too sure how or if my family would have managed.

The emotional and psychological devastation of the fire had taken its toll on our family as a whole. My siblings and I did whatever we could to survive. Once we moved into our first apartment, we realized that times had changed drastically. My parents first apartment after the fire was on the 3rd floor of a 3-family house. It was only a one bedroom in which 6 individuals would live for the next 3 years. Instead of my parents buying furniture from Seeman's, Macy's or Levitz Home Furniture, the Goodwill Mission became our new furniture and appliance store. There we learned the value of second hand goods. The mere thought of something being considered second hand has now begun to excite me. I was pleased to know that someone somewhere had the kind spirit and generosity in their heart to make provisions for me while I was in need. Nearly 40 years have passed and I still get emotional at the thought that someone gave so that I could have.

It is because of organizations like the Salvation Army, American Red Cross and the Goodwill Mission that I credit where a lot of my socially conscious origins are maintained. It is clearly due to my parents examples that service within my spirit was birthed from them. It is through their direct impact that my mantra "Leave More Than You Take" resonates within the hearts of many people today. I'm sure somewhere within me I would have still matured with a philanthropic spirit of giving in spite of the fire that my family experienced. Over the years I've seen countless times where the Salvation Army came to the aid of disaster victims around the country. Even as a child and not really being able to make the connection, my mom would instruct us to put change into the red bucket as the Salvation Army Officers stood outside the supermarket where we shopped. Back then, I could have never imagined that today I'd be a Trustee on the Board of that same organization.

One can never be certain as to the direction of their life's journey. You can start off, as some may view, behind the eight ball and end up as an executive of a major corporation. A large part of that result is determined by how you view yourself and the world in which you live. As for my journey, I had a very low self-esteem. I allowed the negative influences to take their toll on me. I internalized everything, causing more physical and psychological damage to my spirit than anything else. I took out all of my grievances on myself. I no longer valued the life that God entrusted me to take care of. I was just existing in the world and never understood the beauty of living. I ended up in the hospital and then two years following that 3 weeks stay, I attended extensive outpatient counseling. There were many who mentored and instilled positive affirmations for growth and development while living with severe depression. Dr. Shelly Neiderbach over time reinforced how to develop the confidence to use the tools that I've been given.

Along with Dr. Shelly, it was through the unselfish acts of my mentor Dr. William Howard M. Griffith, that I started to see the world differently. It was Howard who deposited unconditional love and attention. He did this before he knew

Young Men, National Mentoring Camp," he instills independence as well as group leadership skills into the minds of young men across this country. Simultaneously, he established the *"Girls Who Rule The World;"* a camp whose mantra expresses *"Girls, Creating Ladies Mentoring Camp."*

Harvey is just one celebrated individual who understands the principles of service. He chooses to use his many platforms to educate the public on the plight and disparities within the inner cities. Steve is not waving a banner or marching down rioted streets as an activist. What he's doing is being proactive in the betterment of the lives of our youth, by ensuring that they are better equipped academically, socially, and have a better understanding of economic empowerment. It's not only the youth who are affected by his activism, the business communities are influenced as well. A little over 7 years ago, Steve developed and produced an awards show entitled *"The Neighborhood Awards"* or aka *"The Hoodie Awards."* There he used his platform to highlight companies, organizations and individuals who are productive within the inner city communities.

Mr. Harvey is the epitome of service as well as being my mantra in action that charges all of us to *"Leave More Than You Take."* He uses his personal money to establish organizations that benefit the greater good of the community. While money is only part of the equation, he demonstrates that it takes a willingness on the behalf of the individual to serve.

Synonymous to Steve's willingness to serve, I've witnessed acts of service through neighbors who ran and sounded the neighborhood alarm while my house was ablaze, saving countless lives; or those who clothed me and my family as we stood bare curbside. It could be seen in my mentor Dr. Griffith, who sensed that we were up to no good, but still decided to instill into my life, which directly changed my trajectory for the better. How impactful is it to have a stranger see more value in you, than you see in yourself? How cool would it be if more people would adopt the philosophy to *"Leave More Than You Take."* Maybe then we could put an end to poverty, homelessness, and reduce the crime rate that plagues our community. Maybe then we will see more acts of philanthropic efforts and donations by more lay folks. It's amazing to realize that so many of us think that we must to have a lot of money in order to give. This can be seen in the Barack H. Obama's 1st and 2nd Presidential campaign fundraising. Through grassroots fundraising techniques, he encouraged the nation to give small donations. As a result of their commitments, he was able to raise more money during the Presidential election than any of his predecessors. It is in the commitment to others where our charity begins. I have come to accept the fact that it's a personal choice that one has to make for themselves. No one can force another to give. It's purely something that you have to want to do and that's why I cry out loud with a call to arms to *"Leave More Than You Take!"*

UNPACKING ONE ITEM AT A TIME

If you think you are too small to make a difference,
Try sleeping with a mosquito.
Dalai Lama

UNPACKING ONE ITEM AT A TIME

ABOUT THE AUTHOR

WILLIAM MICHAEL BARBEE, an advocate for the Behavioral Health Community has been open about his battles of living with a mental illness. He has been a successful businessman for over 25 years., employing hundreds of residents from the community. He dedicates much of his time to philanthropic causes and to the purposed Principle of Service. He has advocated for the Mental Health Community at the United States Capitol, nationally, and throughout the NJ/NY/Conn Metropolitan Area. This is the first of three Inspirational books that he plans to publish. His previously written novel "Clipped Wings They Do Fly" has been turned into a feature film entitled, "Beyond The Silence." It focuses on the life of a man who has a mental illness and finds himself on trial for a crime in which he doesn't remember committing. It also highlights the arduous task that the prosecutor faces, as he struggles to seek a conviction of a mentally ill man. William has hundreds of unpublished poems that were written during his time in counseling with Shelly Neiderbach PhD. William is a successful filmmaker and documentarian with production credits as Director, Producer, Writer, Executive Producer, Editor and Song Writer. He has been featured on several WABC7NY Entertainment News, local television, national radio, and internet radio programs. He enjoys public speaking where he's able to share with audiences around the country messages on living through one's challenges. He's the recipient of several awards and acknowledgements. Born and reared in Newark, NJ, William Michael continues to give back to the community that has afforded him so much.

UNPACKING ONE ITEM AT A TIME

ACKNOWLEDGEMENTS

I WANT TO OFFER MY GRATITUDE to everyone who helped me bring this project to life. Thank you for being my inspiration!

Mommy, you're my everything!

Martia, Jean, Mark, and Marty, you were my comrades in arms whose side I journeyed.

Ellen Richardson, Bishop Claude & Mother Campbell, Walter & Luethel McNeil, Naomi Brantley, Tommy & Ada Robinson, Ben F. Jones, James J. Williams, Katheryn Brantley, Gertrude Hicks, Bishop Thomas & Mother Martin, Alan Sorrell, Mary Nickleson, Amina Baraka, Sen. Ron Rice, Alice Williams, Elders Chester & Carolyn Demps, Mother Ojetta Webb, Dot Mosley, Ruth Moore, Cong. Donald M. Payne Jr., Lacy & Polly Brunson, Peter & Leslie Levine, Bill Cobbs, Chief Apostle Olive Brown, Jack & Karen Farrell, Pamela Rainey-Fort, Roger J. Lundy Jr, Ella Hinnant, Betty Stevens, Elder Melyn Murphy, Jill Griffith, Bill Duke, Joe & Louise Glover, Pastor Clarence Wright, Sylvia Riskin PhD, Lisa Nichols, Bill Cobbs, Mrs. Ruby Young, Bishop Ronald & Toni Bryant Sr., Steven G. & Evelyn Barbee, Bishop H. Eugene Bellinger, Bishop Donald Hilliard, Samuel D. Pollard, Hon. Mildred Crump, Dr. Helen Hoch, Carol Jenkins, Bishop Minerva Bell, Valera Durant, Arthur Wright, Mr. & Mrs. Armando & Gladys Cruz, Barbara Hilbert, and every other mentor who blessed me throughout the years, Thank you!

Coy LaVerne Brantley Curry, LaDonna P. Young, Constance G. Walker, Tanya Elise Shearin-Redman, Wade Trevor Rudolph, Donna L. Walker, Tanya Vicks-Barbee, Pastor Paul R. McClendon, Cathryn Devereaux, Natiah Cheraylis Rosario,

Michelle L. Stevens, Azarine Newman, Hon. Angela Renee Garretson, Jill Rogers, Abigail Adams, Antonio McLendon, Abu NaSeer Muhammad DeLoach, Robin Durant-Harris, Hope Demps Esq, Anita L. Clark, Kimora Jones, Peter Dabrowski MD, Keith Sheppard, Beth A. Kelly, Suzanne Webb Estrella, Jada Barbee, Vanessa Newton, Scott Seale & Frank Ippolito, Kim Armstrong, John Turan, Davelean Porterfield, Angela Dixie, Tiffany Williams-Moore, Dupre Kelly, Jose Manuel Cruz, Phoebe Smith-Hinton, Wincey Terry-Bryant, John C. Arnold, Cynthia M. Vaughan, Dwayne Richardson, Trenee Douglas-Singletary, Joy A. Williams, Jerry A. Casser Esq, James Scott, Lisa McNeil, Toni Henderson-Mayers, Max Beaulieu Esq, Brooke Courtney Kersey, Andrea Holmes Thompkins, Jeff Turan, Bobbi Walston-McCoy, Evett B. Evelyn, LeRoy A. Smith, Terry Williams, Rodney Lewis, Laura Layton, Apryl D. Williams, Sharea Johnson, Barbara Benjamin-Brantley, Bridget Roberts, Salvatore Restifo, Carole Robinson, Richard "Ric" Thigpen Esq, JaNai Monique Fort, Genee Antoinette Dozier Smith, Joe DiStefano, Shawn Bishup Herbert, Gia Compton Esq, Shawn Barbee-Mitchell, Tony Turan, Heidi B. Fuller, Vaughn A. Rosario, James Womack, Syndee Winters, Ana Carril-Grumberg, De Lacy Davis, Francine Williams, Bishop Timothy Pernell, Wayne Johnson, Dr. Antoinette Ellis-Williams, Carol Smith, Tobias Truvillion, Pete Michael Thomas, Sen. Cory Booker, Dr. Asaph C. Womack, you have all been my inspiration! I appreciate you!

Robert Davison, thanks for believing!

Leslie D. Cleveland, thanks for your friendship and proofing this piece.

Kimberly Shamberger, thanks for your commitment to excellence. I can only imagine how complicated the editing process must have been.

**Mental Health Association
of Essex and Morris Counties**
33 S. Fullerton Ave.
Montclair, NJ 07042
973-509-9777
www.mhaessexmorris.org

**Airmid Foundation Inc
Airmid Counseling Services, LLC**
137 Evergreen Pl. Suite 2D
East Orange, NJ 07018
www.airmidfoundation.com

Zion Holy Church
103 Camden St.
Newark, NJ 07103
www.mtsinaichurch.org

Salvation Army
430 Main St.
East Orange, NJ 07018
www.salvationarmyusa.org

Health Care Foundation of the Oranges
80 S. Munn Ave.
East Orange, NJ 07018
www.hcfoinc.org

Montclair Art Museum African American Cultural Committee
3 S. Mountain Ave.
Montclair, NJ 07042
www.montclairartmuseum.org

UNPACKING ONE ITEM AT A TIME

To contact the author, write:
Prestige/Airmid/United
137 Evergreen Pl. Suite 1A
East Orange, NJ 07018

Or call: 1-973-678-3022, (f) 1-973-678-1177

Email: barrichinc@aol.com

www.williammichaelbarbee.com

To Order Books:

www.amazon.com
www.barnesandnoble.com

UNPACKING ONE ITEM AT A TIME

UNPACKING ONE ITEM AT A TIME

CPSIA information can be obtained
at www.ICGtesting.com
Printed in the USA
BVHW032104290322
632756BV00003B/47